INSPIRE YOUR HOME

INSPIRE YOUR HOME

EASY, AFFORDABLE IDEAS TO MAKE EVERY ROOM GLAMOROUS

FARAH MERHI

Tiller Press

New York   London   Toronto   Sydney   New Delhi

TILLER PRESS

An Imprint of Simon & Schuster, Inc.
1230 Avenue of the Americas
New York, NY 10020

First Tiller Press hardcover edition October 2019

TILLER PRESS and colophon are trademarks of Simon & Schuster, Inc.

For information about special discounts for bulk purchases, please contact Simon &
Schuster Special Sales at 1-866-506-1949 or business@simonandschuster.com.

The Simon & Schuster Speakers Bureau can bring authors to your live event.
For more information or to book an event, contact the Simon & Schuster Speakers
Bureau at 1-866-248-3049 or visit our website at www.simonspeakers.com.

Jacket and Interior design by Melissa Clark
Photography by David Sparks Photography
Except on pages 134, 142, 200, 206, 207, photography by
David Burgess from Studio 616 Photography
And on pages 48 and 258, photography by Karyn May Photography

Manufactured in the United States of America

1 3 5 7 9 10 8 6 4 2

Library of Congress Cataloging-in-Publication Data has been applied for.

ISBN 978-1-9821-3124-1
ISBN 978-1-9821-3125-8 (ebook)

DEDICATION

To my children, Celine, Julia, and Adam: If there is one thing I want you to take away from this, it is that when you do what you love from your heart, dreams do come true. You three are my reason, my why, my everything.

To my husband, William: You have shown me the definition of true love. The way you believe in me, the way you're there for me, has allowed me to spread my wings and do what I love without holding back. Thank you for being you. I love you!

To my parents, who sacrificed so much for me growing up, and taught me that hard work and drive are all I need for success, and that being respectful and compassionate toward others is everything I need to be the best version of myself. You continue to be my support system to this day. I am forever grateful, and I love you!

To my mom, who showed me the importance of loving my home. Through you, I learned that our home should be our pride and joy, and that it's one way to take care of our family.

To my fans, customers, and social media friends, you are my extended family, and I will forever be grateful to you for accepting me for who I am and allowing me into your homes whether through investing in my products or through social media. I am forever humbled!
WE did it!

CONTENTS

INTRODUCTION

WOW! • Is this real?

It's still hard for me to believe where I am today. I started Inspire Me! Home Decor in 2012 as a spontaneous idea, a potential outlet for a person who was struggling to find her place in the world. Back then, I was looking for an answer to the not-so-trivial question: What am I meant to do with my life?

I had what you might consider an unusual childhood. I'm Lebanese American, but I grew up in Kinshasa, in the Congo. My father was a businessman, and my mom stayed home to take care of my brother, my sister, and me. Like other African countries, there was a lot of political upheaval. We frequently had to grab what we could carry on our backs and run to the airport due to a military coup or uprising. My childhood was disrupted quite a few times: Leaving Kinshasa meant abandoning our family's home, leaving behind cherished items. But once things settled down, we'd return to start all over again, which I believe played a huge part in instilling a strong will and determination in me. My mom would pick a new house, and no matter what state it was in, within a few months she would turn it into a beautiful home for our family. Watching her start from scratch and make her vision a reality is something that stayed with me. I didn't realize how much of an impact it had on me until I had a home of my own.

I was always opinionated and strong-minded, and from the time I was young I thought I wanted be a lawyer. But, after I went to college in Michigan and prepared to apply to law school, I realized I was just going through the motions. I wasn't truly excited by the idea of studying the law. I knew deep down that being a lawyer wasn't going to make me happy. I summoned my courage and told my family I needed some more time to figure out what I wanted to do.

1

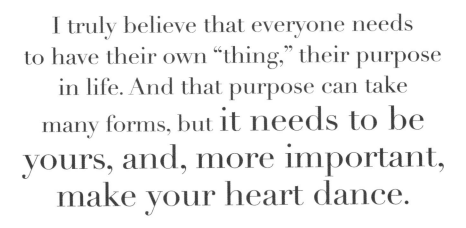

I truly believe that everyone needs to have their own "thing," their purpose in life. And that purpose can take many forms, but it needs to be yours, and, more important, make your heart dance.

A couple of years passed. By all standards, I had an amazing life. A devoted husband, beautiful kids who filled my time, loving parents, extended family and friends. I felt guilty even acknowledging something was missing. Believe me when I say I asked myself over and over, wondering how—in spite of all I had—I could continue to feel a tug, a pull, a NEED for something more. I wanted a career that would make me happy, to love something I could do for myself. Now, don't get me wrong, my family certainly makes me happy, but I truly believe that everyone needs to have their own "thing," their purpose in life. And that purpose can take many forms, but it needs to be yours, and, more important, make your heart dance.

In 2012, we embarked on our first home renovation. I turned to Instagram in search of ideas, but I couldn't find a page that really spoke to me. Maybe it was the mix of my Lebanese heritage and American influence, maybe it was the example my mother had set, but I didn't see my design aesthetic—which I started to identify as "Glam Elegance with a Cozy Vibe"—reflected on the many home decor pages that were out there. I wanted to create a stylish statement home that would also feel warm and inviting; a home that could wow guests and also accommodate my everyday family life.

I decided to share my own process and vision, and nervously launched the Inspire Me! Home Decor Instagram account (@inspire_me_home_decor). I initially didn't tell anyone about it; it was my secret, my creative outlet. I thought I would find a few fellow homeowners who might appreciate any advice and inspiration I discovered along the way. What I found was my calling.

As the renovation progressed, I realized I was waking up each morning energized and ready to tackle the day's to-do list. From picking out paint colors to selecting carpeting, choosing finishes and, most important, bringing my vision to life, I enjoyed making the kind of decisions that tend to frustrate normal people. And, thanks to my growing group of followers, I learned I had a decorating style that seemed to resonate with others. Yes, I embraced bling, faux fur, and metallics. I really loved mirrored pieces, chandeliers, and other statement decor. But I balanced the aspirational with the practical, mixing in pillows, blankets, storage solutions, and other accessories to add coziness and color.

Six months later, our home renovation was done and I looked at my husband and said, "This is what I want to do." I knew I wanted to help others with the home design process. Seven years later here I am, still pinching myself that this is real.

This book is obviously about helping you love and enjoy your home, but it's also about sharing what I've learned on my journey. My goal is to help inspire and encourage you to follow your passion and dreams no matter how scary it may seem. The unknown can be terrifying, but I encourage you to dig deep and build the courage to take that first step. Walk away from the fear bubble and toward what could be your own success story.

If you're to take anything away from this book, it's that living our best lives starts in our home. The sense of inner peace a beautifully decorated and organized home offers will allow you to feel fulfilled and inspired to tackle your day. I want you to feel empowered to bring to life your own interpretation of what your ideal home looks like. No rules, just a helping hand to get you on the way to decorating a home that is a reflection of who you are, your style, and your taste.

Please know that I don't take you for granted: You're my client, my customer, and the reason I'm here. Inspire Me! Home Decor continues to grow, thanks to you. You have honored me with your loyalty, compassion, and encouragement and I will forever be grateful. You are a huge part of this journey, standing by me, crying with me, laughing with me, and cheering me on. We have formed a friendship, a sisterhood if you will, and you inspire me.

When anyone asks me, "What makes an entrepreneur or business owner successful?" I say, "Drive, passion, hard work, and believing in yourself and your goals." That makes for an unstoppable combination. The rewards are beyond what you'll ever imagine. Try it, you'll see.

1
HOME

HOME

I would like you to take a moment. Close your eyes. Inhale, exhale, and say the word *Home*. How does it make you feel? What emotions come up? For me, when I think of "home," I think of my safe place. It's not just a roof over my head but a space designed with love that reflects my taste, style, and personality. When I walk into my home, I feel at peace, no matter what kind of day it's been. Even with the periodic chaos, thanks to my husband, our three kids, and our typically hectic schedule, home is the one place I can't wait to get back to, no matter where I am or what I'm going through. And it's because I designed it to make my family and me happy.

My mom and my grandmother taught me the importance of caring for your home. "Your home should be your pride and joy," my mom would say. She always went the extra mile to bring her vision to life in every home we lived in (if you've read this book's introduction, you'll know we moved a lot). It used to confuse me. "Why so much effort?" I'd ask her. "All we need is furniture to sit on and beds to sleep in, and we're set."

Previous page: More often than not, fireplaces are the focal point of a room. If your fireplace needs a spruce up, change out the tile to something eye-catching and unique like a mirror or a fun mosaic tile that will surely make a statement. A quick and easy update that will make your fireplace the "wow factor" in the room!

Opposite: Glam does not have to mean untouchable. You can have a glamorous, elegant home and still have it look and feel warm and inviting, cozy and livable.

When you love your home, it will love you back.

Then I would visit a friend's house and notice that the parents had, in fact, done just that—invested in furniture and little else. Walking through those rooms made me feel . . . well, I didn't *feel* anything. There was no personality. The house seemed uninviting. I'd go back to our home and notice the difference: In every corner there was a beautiful vignette to look at, a cozy styling to enjoy, and other small details like fresh flower arrangements, candles, or the way my mom would serve her guests coffee in unique-looking mugs with beautifully styled trays of snacks. Visitors would leave feeling loved and appreciated. That's how I learned that if you invest the time and energy, your home will make you and others feel special. It's not about how much you spend, it's about how much thought you put into it, the little touches. Give it love, and it will show you love; neglect it, and stress and anxiety will ensue.

So what do I mean when I say "Make your house a home"? When I think of a house, I think of a structure or building that has yet to be given any attention. A home is born when you fill that structure with your style and personal touch. It's given life when you design it, organize it, and decorate it to reflect and share who you are and what you love. It's a place you walk out of every morning feeling a sense of inner peace and walk back into and breathe a sigh of relief. Your home should be a sanctuary, a place that is unique to you. A place you've showered with love to reflect everything you enjoy. It's not about how big or spacious your home is, it's about the care and personal touches you sprinkle throughout. It's the little things that make a big impact, and what your family and guests will appreciate. Design and styling are what make a house a home.

And now the big question: HOW do you make your house a home? Believe me, I understand it can feel overwhelming and stressful. Where to begin? What are the rules? How do you start figuring out your style, or if things work together?

Okay, first . . . DEEP BREATH. Decorating *can* feel overwhelming but it really doesn't have to be. It's a matter of figuring it out one step at a time. Think of it as a layering process: You have to start with the foundation and gradually add in other details to finish off the look.

The key is don't rush it. There's no time limit. Hopefully you'll be in your home for many years to come. Shifting your mentality and *embracing the process* is essential to becoming more productive (and relaxed) when decorating your dream home. Decorating is about trial and error. Think of getting dressed and how you try on outfits until you find a combination that works. The same concept applies to designing a home. You WILL make mistakes. (Repeat after me: "I WILL make mistakes and that's okay!") It's absolutely fine to keep changing things out until you've found the right piece that makes you feel like you have completed a room (more on this on the next page). And, wow, when a room is finally done, it's an amazing feeling of accomplishment and pride!

With this book, I'm not here to give you rules or lecture you on what your home should look like. I believe a home should be a reflection of individual taste and work for you and your family. But I would like to share my process and philosophy: that beauty can meet function in an affordable way. I am here to encourage you to achieve the look you want and to hold your hand and tell you, "If I can do it, so can you." Let this be a fun ride. Enjoy it—don't let it stress you out.

In addition, I'm going to share with you ways to keep your home organized and clean. I have weekly and seasonal rituals and rewards that I hope will help inspire your cleaning routines.

I'm here to promote the idea of loving and enjoying your home to the fullest. Everyone should be able to make their home a source of pride and joy for their family, a place to create lasting memories.

CAN A COUPLE WHO LIVES TOGETHER DESIGN TOGETHER?

There are three types of home design couples:

1. The couple in which one person makes all the home design decisions.
2. The couple in which both people work hand in hand to design their dream home.
3. The couple who can't seem to agree on anything, which usually results in a permanent state of home design limbo.

Since I like to preach how important designing your home is for your peace of mind, who am I to let number three's situation continue any longer? I'm here to help!

I've worked with couples who struggle to design their home because their opinions cancel each other out. I think that type of mutual veto power is unproductive. I've found that this usually happens because one partner can't visualize how the *finished* room will look and reacts to one piece of furniture or detail they're trying to decide on. They don't have the ability to envision the overall picture. As we know, it's not just a sofa or wall color that makes a room. It's all the pieces coming together along with finishing decor touches.

Here is what I've found to be a productive way of resolving this conundrum.

1. Have a serious conversation as a couple. Ask yourselves what is important for *each* of you before you embark on remodeling or redesigning a room. Write these points down.
2. Find inspirational pictures to help yourselves better understand and visualize what the finished look could be. This will help you both to trust the process instead of going through it blindly.
3. Decide together if one of you can take charge of the project with the other's full support. Ask for patience and for the other to wait until the room is done before rendering a final judgment.
4. Remember that you both live in your home, so it's essential that each of you gets a chance to incorporate what is important to you. There are ways to compromise without taking away from the overall vision.

For example, if there's a tug-of-war between feminine and masculine touches, marry them! (See what I did there?) For instance, if a leather sofa is important to him but a glam look is important to her, bring in a leather sofa that has sleek curves to soften the look. Or if he has a leather couch from his bachelor days that he refuses to part with, add pillows with velvet fabric or beading to soften its look. And consider a beautiful crystal chandelier that will add the glam you're looking for. It's about compromise and working together to balance out your styles. IT CAN BE DONE!

Believe it or not, my husband and I went through a "stuck" phase. He had strong opinions on what he wanted our home to look like. We could not decide which sofas to buy for our family room and were at an impasse for two months. I finally sat him down and told him that he had to trust me. And if he didn't like it after I was done, then we could have a conversation about how we could design our home moving forward. A few weeks later, after I was done furnishing and decorating the room, my husband decided he would never doubt my vision again. Now I can't even get him to give me an opinion. "Honey, should I get this dining table?" Him: "Whatever you think will work." Not because he has given up, but because I showed him that I knew what I was doing and was taking his needs into consideration.

At the end of the day, when you walk through those doors, make sure your home feels like the sanctuary you deserve to escape the reality of your daily life. Let it embrace you with its warmth and welcome you into a cozy space. Let it be the place where you feel safe, the place that sparks love and joy in your heart, the place you've poured your soul into so you can find a sense of peace in your own corner of heaven. Home is where my heart is; it's where I make memories with my children, who will one day look back and wave goodbye as they move on with their lives. It's the place where I'll grow old with my husband, where I've had laughter, sadness, happiness, and everything in between. It's where I dealt with tough times in my life, where I found myself, where I learned so much about myself. It's where I can be me, surrounded by love and acceptance. Home is love.

WHERE TO BEGIN?

Decorating your home can be overwhelming and stressful, especially if you have no idea where to start. Before I share my tips, please remember: Your mind-set here is critical.

Just like anything in life, if you are going to embark on something new feeling anxious, then it will be hard for the experience NOT to feel difficult and draining. You should try to approach this project with an open mind and willingness to embrace the process. Shift your thinking from *This is going to be hard and overwhelming* to *This is going to be fun. What a blessing that I get to decorate and furnish my home!* You, with your own hands and your own personal touch, are about to make your house a home to enjoy—what's not to like about that?

Keep your eye on the prize. If you make a mistake, consider it a teachable moment and then course correct. Nothing is set in stone. Paint color wasn't what you expected? So what, repaint! Wrong sofa? Move it to another room or return it! Rug is too small? Oh well, exchange it for the right size! Pillows aren't working? Try different sizes and styles until you get it the way you feel is right! Don't be hard on yourself. I've made many mistakes and learned from them.

How do you start furnishing and decorating a room? One step at a time! Remember to think of this as a layering process. First, try to pinpoint what style you envision for your home. Have you figured out a look you love? It's nice to have the same aesthetic flow from room to room. No matter what kind of house you live in (open floor plan or traditional), it's all under one roof so cohesiveness is key. If you know the style you want to go with, then great—you're ready to move to the next step. If you are unsure and can't decide which style you're drawn to, that's okay: Visual aids always help.

WHAT IS THE DEFINITION OF GLAM ELEGANCE?

In my mind, there are many ways to interpret "glamour," but only one way to interpret "elegance." So to me, Glam Elegance really translates to "glamorously understated." It's represented in a home that's elegantly styled, meaning it's easy on the eye and enjoyable to spend time in. It relies on timeless and classic elements but still makes a statement with glamorous touches. Glam elegance is achievable, livable, cozy, and inviting.

I personally think you can infuse glam into just about any style:

1. Modern Glam
2. Farmhouse/Rustic Glam
3. Industrial Glam (not pictured)
4. Transitional Glam
5. Traditional Glam

Q: Can I mix and match my coffee table and side tables?

A: YASS! In fact, I highly recommend you do! A mirrored coffee table with marble side tables . . . mmm, gorgeousness! A glass coffee table and wooden side tables? Absolutely, yes! A wooden coffee table and mirrored side tables, an ottoman and wooden side tables . . . Okay, you get the picture! Excitement gets the better of me.

ELEGANCE IS WHEN
THE INSIDE IS AS
THE OUTSIDE
- COCO CHANEL

FAQ

Q: How do I infuse glam touches into a room that is already furnished?

A: You can always add a touch of glam to what you already have. Easy ideas include: adding pillows or blankets with faux fur or metallic print and threads; incorporating mirrored or Lucite pieces into a room (think console, side table, coffee table, lamps); and, of course, there's always the option of adding a crystal chandelier. See the above Before and After pictures: this condo rental already had furniture in it. The feel was very modern, with a touch of an industrial vibe. Because it was a smaller space, I wanted to stick to a light color palette. Maximizing storage and seating was essential, too. Because it's a rental, we couldn't change the lighting, but everything else got a touch of glam!

MY APPROACH STEP-BY-STEP

I'll be going over my approach room by room in the following chapters, but in general my "layering" process starts by determining the big picture (wall color and major furniture pieces), and then moving step-by-step toward accent decor.

STEP #1:

Paint

Here's the good thing about paint: If you're not happy with the color, it can easily be repainted. There is also a way to play around with paint and decide on the right shade before committing to a whole room in a particular color (more on this later). But don't be afraid to go with fun, bold paint in areas of your home. If you choose to go with dark tones, balance things out with lighter furniture. If you do not want to commit to a dark color for a whole room, I would suggest thinking about an "accent wall" or "feature wall." This means painting one wall a dark or bright shade (to provide a focal point), and painting the rest of the room in a lighter shade of the same color family. For example, paint your accent wall a dark shade of gray and then the rest of your room in a lighter gray. I have always loved going with lighter wall paint in my main living spaces. I am drawn to bright rooms so I tend to choose lighter paint with warm undertones for a cozy feel.

Wallpaper

We are lucky to live in a world where removable wallpaper is a thing! (Can I get a WOOT! WOOT!) Yes, it's true: Removable wallpaper allows you to apply it to your walls, and, whenever you want a change, you can easily peel it off without any residue left behind. Gone are the days of tedious wallpaper application and removal! How do I know this? I had the brilliant idea of removing old wallpaper myself in our powder room. Let's just say that our painters advised me to please never attempt that again. Full disclosure: I have my own line of removable wallpaper with Tempaper and have used it around my home. So I speak from personal experience when I say it's the way to go! I'm here to say have fun with wallpaper, my friends! Whether it be a feature wall or a full room, look for removable wallpaper and don't hold back!

STEP #2:

Big-Ticket Items

Big-ticket items include sofas, beds, kitchen cabinets, rugs—the pieces that are long-term investments, or can't be easily switched out. This includes thinking about:

Color Palette

If you're like me and love to spruce up your home by switching out your color palette every few months, you may want to stick to neutral-colored furniture: gray, beige, tan, ivory, white, black, and brown. Having neutral fabrics for your major furniture pieces allows you to easily update your room through your accessories and accent decor without putting a dent in your bank account.

Scale

When furnishing a room, keep in mind the space you have. Take measurements before buying furniture to make sure it's the right fit. Don't crowd your room with oversized furniture, or buy furniture that is too small for the space. Eyeballing and buying a lamp is one thing (and easily exchanged), but eyeballing big furniture pieces is another story (more expensive and a hassle). Scale is important for everything you add to a room. A small light fixture in a big space will feel lost, while a large coffee table in a smaller room will crowd your space and make it hard for you to walk around easily and comfortably.

Here's an example: Someone from my "Insta Fam" shared a picture of her bedroom with me. The room is huge, and she did a beautiful job of furnishing and styling it. But my eyes kept focusing on the small lamps on her nightstands. They felt out of place, dwarfed by the furniture and the grandeur of the room. It was so noticeable I couldn't appreciate the rest of her bedroom. I gently pointed this out to her and suggested she change them out for bigger/taller lamps. A few days later, she sent me a picture of her bedroom with new lamps and, suddenly, the room felt cohesive and I could take it all in.

Rug size

For a better visual and to ensure your furniture does not slip and move around in a room, make sure you invest in a rug that will lie at least halfway under a furniture piece. The front legs of your furniture should be resting on the rug. If you can fit all your furniture on the rug, then even better!

When it comes to your dining room, you'll want a rug large enough so that your table and dining chairs can all sit fully on top of it.

STEP #3:

Accent Pieces

Accent pieces can be armchairs, side tables, consoles, coffee tables, benches, lamps, light fixtures, etc.

Always feel free to mix and match pieces that you may be buying more than one of to add personality and visual appeal. I especially like to mix different side tables; I can easily move them from one room to another if I feel like it's time to change things up.

If you have a favorite color and are certain it's one you'll like for a long time, then splurge on armchairs in that color! Armchairs (or pillows) are a little easier to replace than a sofa. For example, I love cobalt blue. I've been drawn to it for years. So I decided to infuse that color into my formal living room.

A light fixture or chandelier makes a statement and ties the room together. Here is an opportunity for you to add a wow factor to your room and get away with it not feeling overly done. As glam as you go with your light fixture, considering your furniture and accent pieces, it all balances out.

STEP #4:

Power Accessories

I absolutely love pillows and throw blankets. They offer so much textural variety and color, and can instantly elevate or soften a room. I rely on these power accessories year-round to add pops of color, infuse touches of glam, or make a room cozier.

STEP #5:

Accent Decor

This is my favorite category: decorative boxes, bowls, trays, candles, vases, flower arrangements, wall art, window treatments, etc.

It's all in the details! Those are what make a room. I know I sound like a broken record, but man oh man is it true. I can't tell you how many times a day I say that.

Styling your coffee table and side tables with accent decor infuses a personal touch that makes your home YOURS. What's a room without the details? It's just a room. No personal touch, no personality. And this is where I always say, *Have fun with it!* There are so many different decor pieces like trays, vases, candlesticks, and decorative boxes for you to love and choose from!

I often use the family room as an example, so allow me to share another—the kitchen, possibly everyone's favorite room! When I walk into a kitchen that has bare surfaces, I think, *Here's a kitchen that's missing personality.* There's no need to overcrowd your counters, but adding a few decanters, a fresh floral arrangement, or a pretty bowl is enough to add a personal touch and takes your kitchen from bare to fabulous!

Window treatments

Two questions I get asked a lot are where and how do I hang my curtains. I love the dramatic look you get from hanging curtains as high as possible. Two options you could consider:

1. Hang your rod halfway between the top of the window and the ceiling.
2. Hang your rod as close to the ceiling as possible.

What about the bottom, you ask? Think floor-length or puddle! In my family room (pictured at right), which has a very high ceiling, drapes provide that dramatic sweep while adding warmth and texture. In a room with standard-height ceilings, curtains can help provide the illusion of higher ceilings if you hang them high.

There are many ready-made curtain panels available. Remember to measure before heading out to shop. Decide where you want to hang your rod, then choose between the available options for you: 84 inches, 96 inches, or 108 inches long. You can always have the curtains hemmed a bit if needed. Depending on where you're shopping, you may need to go the custom route if you need panels longer than 96 inches. Most stores carry curtains up to 96 inches long, though some may sell panels online that are up to 108 inches long.

Although custom drapes can get a bit pricey, consider them an investment in your home, preventing the sun from fading your floors and furniture. I had to completely change my furniture a few years back due to the sun fading the fabric on my sofa and armchairs. It's a thing, I promise! Drapes also offer peace of mind by allowing for privacy.

If you're considering curtains, then you'll also need to think about curtain hardware (rods, hooks, and tie-backs). These come in a range of materials and colors like brass, brushed nickel, or wood, and are some examples of how you can customize the look of your window treatments to complete the aesthetic you're going for in each room.

If you're decorating a small room that could benefit from light and doesn't require privacy, then you can always aim for a minimalist look and keep your windows bare. Remember, it's all about how you feel walking into your home. Do what makes you happy—incorporate ideas that will make you smile when relaxing in your space.

Always remember to think of styling as a fun process.
Take your time and layer in your furniture and decor step-by-step to avoid feeling overwhelmed.

HOW TO USE THIS BOOK

Starting with the next chapter, I will walk you through all the rooms of the house. We'll begin with the big picture and then narrow in with step-by-step photos of everything from arranging a blanket to styling shelves. The vision for this book is to hold your hand through the process and give you the tools and inspiration you need to help make your house a home. I want you to be able to come back to this book as many times as you need. Whether you are embarking on designing your home now or at some point down the road, this book is meant to "be there for you." Style it on your coffee table, shelf, or console for a layering look or a special decor piece, and reference it when questions come up. Feeling uninspired and need a little boost to get you going? That's what all these pictures are for. From a designer who cherishes her home and believes it should spark a sense of peace within, I hope you'll find my book helpful, lighthearted, and fun to read! Above all, I hope it will make you smile and feel inspired. Are you ready to have some fun with me? What are we waiting for? On to Chapter 2 we go!

2

ENTRYWAY & MUDROOM

ENTRYWAY & MUDROOM

ften overlooked or neglected, your entryway and/or mudroom is the first room(s) your guests will see when they enter your home. It's easy to assume other areas of the house should take priority, but think of your first impression when you walk into other people's homes. Is it impacted by the way the entryway is decorated? Or how the mudroom is organized and styled? I think it's important that these areas be visually appealing and welcoming. They should also provide a sneak peek of what's inside the rest of the house, so design consistency is key.

Now, you may be thinking, *Come on Farah, the entryway is a small space, how much of an impact can it actually have?* The answer is so much, my friends! Not only for your guests, but, most important, for yourself! At the end of each day, when you walk into your home, why not feel welcomed? Your home will help you relax if you can walk into an area with instant visual appeal.

Let's start with the entryway and then move on to the mudroom.

Previous page: With a two-story ceiling, my entryway needs decor that can fill up all the empty space. So in the corner, I styled a floor vase with tall, natural branches. Stores are offering more and more options to make your space feel unique.

HIGHLIGHTS

A durable rug goes a long way

Make these rooms feel welcoming yet functional

You can never go wrong with fresh flowers and a candle

REMEMBER

Your entryway should be a representation of your entire home, so give this room as much attention as you give the rest of your home. Try to make your mudroom look good but also be functional, so you and your family can easily walk in and not only feel at home but also have access to storage solutions to help keep your everyday essentials organized.

CHECKLIST FOR ENTRYWAY SUCCESS

○ Most entryways don't get a lot of natural lighting; paint your walls a lighter shade to brighten up the room.

○ A rug is a must.

○ Wall art and mirrors are always a plus.

○ Add a statement light fixture.

Opposite: If you have a two-story entryway, you can hang additional items higher up on your walls to avoid their looking bare. Whether you go with candles or artwork or wall decor, make sure they complement the other pieces in the room for a cohesive look.

When I think of an entryway, I think of a sneak peek . . . a teaser of what's to come.

Don't feel that your creativity must be limited when designing in a small area. Use every space you can to make a statement. Small things can make a big impact.

ENTRYWAY

When it comes to your entryway, remember: It should reflect all the time and energy you put into designing the rest of your home. It doesn't need to be as functional as your mudroom, so the focus should be on visual appeal. From statement light fixtures to mirrors or even a seating area, this is a space where you can get creative and focus on impressing your guests as they enter your home.

My entryway is an awkward space: It's narrow with a tall ceiling, lots of doorways, and a staircase wall. Styling and decorating it was definitely a challenge. I had to strategize about what I wanted to put there while avoiding making the space feel too cramped or too empty. I had to find the right balance. I knew I wanted a console to style with decorative accents, and, because of the high ceiling, a statement chandelier.

Opposite: This wall gave me enough space to add a small console. I chose a mirrored console to reflect light and give an illusion of a bigger space. (This is one of my favorite tricks to use when working with smaller rooms.)

The space above the console felt bare and empty. I wanted to add something fun and decorative. I styled a piece of wall decor that fit perfectly in this spot, keeping in mind the color, size, and design as I put it together.

This faux fur stool was the final touch I needed to add texture and warmth in this area!

I remember when we were shopping for a home, my husband and I walked into the foyer of this house and the first thing that welcomed us was the smell of warm vanilla. It was a candle burning in the foyer. All I could think about after that was how that smell made me think of "home." I felt warm inside, and it put a smile in my heart and on my face. I envisioned us spending time in the kitchen, cooking and baking. I envisioned us spending time in the family room, laughing and building memories. I was sold! All that—from a burning candle—sparked emotions through my senses. I never underestimated the power of a candle again.

Opposite: If you have a space that feels empty, like this wall and corner, fill it with art or a mirror and bench if you can fit one. On this wall, I mounted a piece of art that was made for me by my friend Mary from Copper Corners. I then added a bench from my furniture collection. And, of course, pillows and a throw for styling! We now have a place to sit and put on our shoes before walking out the door.

Every entryway needs a rug that can withstand heavy foot traffic (like jutte, sisal, or a flat weave). We live in snowy and muddy Michigan. I personally don't allow guests into my home with their shoes on, so my rug allows them to take off their shoes without directly touching the floor. I get so many inquiries about how to ask guests to take their shoes off before walking into your home without sounding rude. Well, there's no way around it. The way I see it, it's your home, your rules. I have kids and would rather not have dirt and germs to deal with. So I politely and gently ask my guests if they can leave their shoes at the door because of the kids. You would be surprised at how understanding people can be when you say "kids." You could have extra clean slippers handy for guests to wear when they take their shoes off if you know you have people coming over.

Ladies and gentlemen, allow me to push you to really think outside the box here. Go all out! Make the lighting fixture the piece that embraces you every time you walk into your home. A bit dramatic? I guess, but you get the point! Create drama in this room. Make a statement with your lighting fixture, especially if you have a two-story ceiling. There are so many options out there. Pick one that speaks to your style and design aesthetic. I went with this gorgeous piece that, thanks to its length and finish, ties the whole space together!

Oh, the struggle of keeping our mudroom organized.

With three kids and eight months of bitter cold temperatures, well, it makes for a messy mudroom at all hours of the day. Simply put, winter gear is a pain!

MUDROOM

When it comes to mudrooms, the secret is to strategize before you embark on designing the space. Figure out how the mudroom is going to work for you. Do you have kids? Do you have pets? Do you need storage? Will your guests mainly enter through here? Do you have space for decorative accents? How is the lighting? These are all important factors to keep in mind before designing the space.

Boiling it down, the three things to consider for your mudroom are: storage, functionality, and visual appeal.

This should go without saying: Functional storage is a must. If your mudroom allows, built-in storage is definitely a great investment. My built-in was designed for the space, and has both shelves and hooks. I like to hang our coats for easy access, placing bags and backpacks on the bench, with shoes hidden away underneath.

Don't forget an area rug. Make sure your rug can withstand muddy or wet shoes. A jute rug is always a great option and can handle whatever comes in from the outdoors.

Wicker baskets are great for added storage. I use mine for stowing away winter essentials like hats and gloves, or anything else that tends to collect in piles, like shopping bags or umbrellas.

A mirror is a must-have for last-minute outfit checks before heading out.

CHECKLIST FOR MUDROOM SUCCESS

○ Take stock of the space: If you don't have built-in storage, make do by investing in a shelving unit or purchasing storage furniture like benches or ottomans to store things away. If you don't have a dedicated mudroom, that's okay! Adding a bench with baskets under it can help convert a small place into a dedicated area in your entryway for all your shoes and knickknacks. Hang hooks over your bench for coats and jackets and a dog leash if you have pets. Use the bench to sit and put your shoes on before walking out the door. It's all about getting creative with the space you have.

○ Consider some must-haves: a console table or bench, mirror, rug, and lighting.

○ Storage baskets are a pretty way to store things away.

○ Add decorative elements like artwork or pictures, a plant, a chair, or an umbrella stand if you have the space for them.

Opposite: If your mudroom allows, extra seating in the form of a bench or chair is always good for days your whole family is trying to get out the door at the same time.

Decorative accents are always a great addition to complete the look. Remember to choose pieces that complement the rest of your home for consistency. But if you can't fit decorative accents in your mudroom, don't sweat it. This is the one room where functionality is most important!

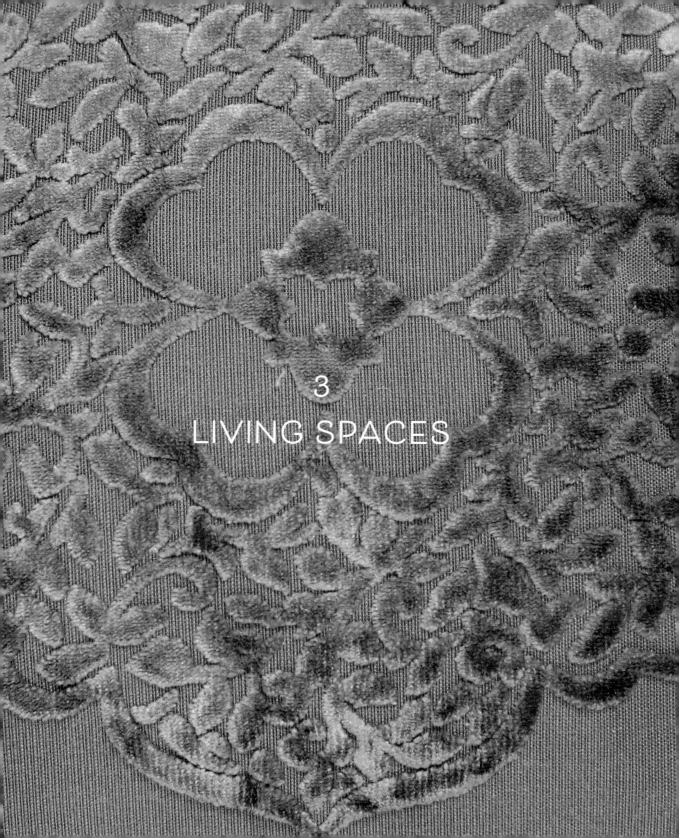

3

LIVING SPACES

LIVING SPACES

In this chapter I'm combining family rooms and living rooms into what I've called "Living Spaces," because I think the ideas here apply to either room (and, for many people, the living room functions as the family room).

Personally, these rooms are my favorite areas to design. They are the rooms where everybody—including adults—gets to hang out, and where we build memories. Whether you're hosting family and friends, enjoying movie night with your kids, playing board games, or just sitting around relaxing, the living or family room brings people together. I love designing them in a way that looks great but is also functional. These rooms should accommodate your kids during your everyday life, but still look sophisticated so you can proudly show them off when you have friends over.

I have heard many people say, "I'll wait until my kids are out of the house to design my dream family or living room." That makes me sad. Life is short, and I believe you can still have a beautiful home to enjoy *while* your kids are in it. For instance, my favorite childhood memories consist of my family and me gathering in our family room to watch a movie or just talk. The way my mom designed and decorated always added to the experience of spending time in there. It felt cozy and warm; it felt loved and uncluttered. At the time, I may not have shown my mom the appreciation she deserved, but how she decorated plays a huge role in the way I design for my family. And, just like my mom, I've set a few ground rules that keep our furniture clean and these rooms tidy!

Having kids shouldn't prevent you from enjoying your home and designing it the way you want. Messes are easy to clean.

HIGHLIGHTS

Embrace kid-friendly solutions, like fabric protection.

Maximize your storage space; think furniture with storage solutions.

Rely on accent pieces to add glamorous touches to your room.

CHECKLIST FOR LIVING SPACES SUCCESS

○ Pick out your sofas (see more on sofas on page 62)

○ Don't underestimate the power of your coffee table
  (see page 65)

○ Pick side chairs and accent colors

○ Rugs and curtains

○ Add functional decor

○ Accent pieces

Opposite: The number one rule in my book is fabric protection for your sofas, chairs, and carpets. Fabric protection will help with easy cleanups. Most furniture stores offer this service when you purchase your seating. If you've already purchased your furniture, you can DIY it and head to your local Home Depot or Lowe's and buy fabric protection spray to apply on your own. If you're like me and would prefer leaving this to the professionals, call a local cleaning company that offers fabric protection treatment.

Get your kids to pitch in by showing them how to clean up after themselves when they're done playing. They'll learn early on the value of maintaining a home and to appreciate a well-kept space.

FLOORING

Looking to change things up? Tile may look grand, but I love the warmth of wood floors. Look into engineered wood or vinyl wood flooring that looks like real wood but can be water- and scratch-resistant.

If you're curious about vinyl flooring, I highly recommend it. I've found it to be a great-looking, durable, wallet-friendly solution. When we remodeled our basement, I knew two things: 1) I didn't want to have to worry about my kids scratching the floors, and 2) We live in a flood zone. The vinyl wood floor by NuCore looks and feels just like wood, but it's waterproof (perfect if you have kids or pets). Also, it's scratch-resistant! We dragged a three-hundred-pound dresser across the room—not a mark.

For my main floor (thinking about resale value), I went with engineered wood. This is not as durable as vinyl, but it's beautiful! Engineered wood floors come in many colors, textures, and widths. Order samples and place them in your room to get a feel for what each color will do for your space. Replacing our old family room carpet with engineered wood was the best decision I ever made. Remember the scene in *Risky Business* where Tom Cruise slides into the room wearing socks but no pants and starts to sing? That was me as soon as my floors were done. (Except I was fully clothed, I promise.)

If you have wood or tile floors, a rug is a great way to bring warmth and coziness into a space. It anchors a room and takes it from looking cold and bare to warm and inviting. (See tips on rug size on page 22.)

CURTAINS

Curtains are another great way to add warmth and texture or soften the look of a room. I like to hang them high, just below the ceiling, and have them just touch the floor. It makes a room feel grander and gives the illusion of higher ceilings.

Q: How do you keep everything from looking too matchy-matchy in your living space?

A: I love this question, because I do get it a lot. I'm often asked how to avoid making a home feel too matchy-matchy, without any character. Think of mixing and matching the finishes on your furniture. Add a pop of color or two. Mix and match your fabrics and textures. Play around with pattern, and, most important, have fun and don't overthink it. Remember, it's all about your home making you feel happy inside, and that's all that should matter here! And just to put it out there: It's totally okay if your home feels matchy-matchy or, in a better description, monochromatic and simple.

SOFAS

When looking for a new sofa or sectional, think about functionality. You want something that looks good but is comfortable so you can actually enjoy sitting on it.

No matter your style, my rule of thumb is to pick a neutral color, such as white, tan, or gray. Sofas are a big investment, and if you go with a neutral color, you'll be able to switch the surrounding color scheme without having to buy brand-new furniture each time. I love to udpate our decor along with the seasons. Or maybe a new color trend is on the rise and I'll feel like infusing that palette throughout the house. Neutral-colored furniture allows me to freshen up our rooms easily without breaking the bank.

COFFEE TABLES

Coffee table options are endless and exciting—there are so many types to choose from! Take the time and invest in a beautiful table that will complement your space. I have a mirrored coffee table, which adds a glam focal point to the room.

Now, I know that if you have kids, your concern is fingerprints and smudges on glass and mirrors. Personally, I don't mind having to wipe down my tables a few times a day if I'm going to get the elegant look a glass or mirrored table will offer. Wood tables can also scratch and stain easily, but don't discount a material based on how dirty it can get—decide what will look good in your space and what's best for your lifestyle. From wood to glass to metal or even a round ottoman, there are many great options to choose from.

Distressed (rustic): You don't have to worry about scratches or dents. More scratches add character! Great choice if you have kids and/or pets.

Double layer: If you're concerned about storage, choose a table that has two layers. Add wicker baskets or crates filled with toys or other items you would like to store and place them on the bottom of the table.

Modern: A metal-and-glass table with clean lines is ideal for a modern-feel living room. It's simple in design but still eye-catching.

Tray tables: These are fun and unique, and work with just about any living room style. They offer a different design from the traditional coffee table, and are definitely eye-catching, right? You can have this look in leather, wood, glass, metal, or mirror.

Glam elegance: Mirrored tables and metallic tables with pattern designs are quite the statement pieces for your living room. If your design style is transitional glam, modern glam, or Hollywood glam, then these are perfect for you. For sharp edges, invest in child-proof corner covers.

Traditional: All wood or a mix of wood and glass, traditional tables have come a long way from looking outdated. They are classic and timeless.

Industrial: Mixed wood and metals can work in modern, farmhouse, and even transitional styles. It's all about balancing things out. You can soften the look with pillows, throws, rugs, and home decor for a nice cohesive flow.

Ottomans can fill in for coffee tables and are a great alternative if you have kids. You won't have to worry about them bumping into them and getting hurt. Available in fabric or leather, ottomans exude an inviting and cozy feel. Use trays to add accent decor or to hold food and drinks.

A collection of square side tables: You can use sets of two, four, or six. When set up next to each other, they function as a coffee table. But you can also pull them apart to create more space when company comes, or use them as side tables for holding drinks and snacks.

FAQ

Q: **How do I decorate a coffee table?**

A: Turn the page to see more, but some staples I swear by are trays, stacked books, candles, and bowls.

STYLING COFFEE & SIDE TABLES

Coffee and side tables provide a little more space for you to create visual focal points and share your personality (when they're not being used to hold snacks and drinks). In addition to flowers and books, I love to add unusual geometric items that draw the eye or invite a question. This is a fun place for you to layer!

The key is mixing and matching and creating vertical or horizontal tableaux. I love to collect glass boxes, vases, and trays—items I can use to stack or group together to create a vignette.

Above: I frequently rely on fresh and faux flowers to add a punch of color and bring a bit of the outdoors inside. Here the gold leaf provides a nice undulating shape but echoes the horizontal direction of the books, so there's a balance between the leaf and books and the canisters and flowers.

Left: Three is the magic number. This table lamp anchors the side table, while the decorative box and mercury candle balance out the space without taking away from the lamp's gorgeous base.

SIDE CHAIRS

Pick an accent color. Look for inspiration and notice what colors you're drawn to. These can be rich, royal colors like plum or cobalt blue, or brighter pops like turquoise and fuchsia. Once you've decided on a color or two, your next step is to select side chairs. From wingback or barrel to classic armchairs, the possibilities are endless. Your side chairs can be patterned and include your pop of color in the fabric, or you can stick to neutrals. Don't be afraid to mix and match fabrics and textures! If your sofa is linen, it's okay to bring in velvet armchairs, and vice versa. Same if you're working with leather, microfiber, or any other type of fabric. Mixing materials is okay.

STORAGE

As I mentioned earlier, storage is key, especially if you have kids. There is no shortage of storage solutions out there! My go-tos are wicker baskets and ottomans. Not only do they look great and complement any space, but they also make it easy to stash away Legos and stuffed animals.

Left: Fill a wicker basket up with added throw blankets and pillows for family movie nights.

Opposite: Poufs also look great and you can use them for added seating!

FUNCTIONAL DECOR

By this I mean side tables for additional surface areas, floor lamps and table lamps to add warmer lighting, and mirrors, which reflect light and make a room feel brighter and more spacious.

I like to mix and match side tables for a personalized look. Or opt for nesting tables! They look cool and double up as extra side tables layered over one another or split up and styled around the room.

Timeless and classic, mirrors or mirrored furniture are here to stay! Mirrors reflect light, make your room feel bright, and give the illusion of a bigger space. (Yes, you'll need to clean fingerprints, but the pros these pieces offer outweigh the cons of extra cleaning.)

Adding table lamps or floor lamps can brighten up a small space or provide a warmer glow for those nights spent curled up on the sofa reading a book or magazine. I can't imagine a room feeling complete without a lamp. Turn on your lamp in the evenings for a warm and cozy feel and go about your night.

Again, it's totally fine to use a mix of materials in one setting. I love mixing it up—not everything has to be matchy-matchy. I know it can feel confusing but don't overthink it. Wood, metal, mirror, and glass in one room make the room look interesting and unique. In fact, it's a trend, and it's here to stay!

ACCENT PIECES

I love to use flowers, vases, candles, jars, boxes, family photos, books, and trays. Pillows and throw blankets can add a pop of color or a cozy touch. Use rich textures, like faux fur and velvet, which is on trend! See page 22 for more tips on how to use and style accents.

Shelving is key to holding decorative accent pieces.

Yes, you'll need to clean fingerprints, but the pros these pieces offer outweigh the cons of extra cleaning.

And consoles act as nice dividers between rooms.

HOW TO STYLE A THROW BLANKET

I love using throw blankets to add coziness, color, and texture to a room (and, of course, to wrap myself in while reading or watching TV!). I use faux fur and velvet throws for dramatic effect, along with more traditional wool or cotton blankets. In fact, my kids and I used to fight over who gets which blanket, so I always have extra ones stashed away in our storage ottomans for when we are all in the family room enjoying a movie. (Hands off my blanket!)

The "effortless drape" look: I gather one end of the blanket over the sofa arm, and fan the other end on the floor. This faux fur throw adds an inviting, luxurious touch, while the stripe pattern echoes the painting on the wall.

A half roll: Here's another dramatic way to display a blanket, with one end rolled up so it can rest on the sofa seat. This blue velvet provides a strong pop of color and helps draw your eye to the center of the couch.

Drape a blanket on the back of a sofa to add interest to your sofa if the back is facing another living space.

Baskets are always a great way to store blankets, but sometimes I like to let them peek out so kids or guests know where to find them, and it makes for a great styling!

The simple rectangle fold: Here I just fold the blanket lengthwise and drape it over the chair, displaying any fringe or trim in the front. I like how the white blanket is hardly visible against the white chair but emphasizes the chair's vertical line while providing an invitation to sit.

SEASONAL CHANGES

If you follow me on social media, you know how much I enjoy changing things out for the seasons. Reflecting what's going on outdoors in my home allows me to redecorate and keeps my home from feeling like it needs a spruce up. I love changing out my color palette completely! In this room, I've gone from bold and neutral to cozy plum and lavender tones (pages 90–91) to bold cobalt blue and gold (pages 92–93)! Let's just say, my husband has stopped looking surprised every time he walks into a revamped room. I then go around and change out my scented candles to candles with scents that reflect the season. A few more seasonal decor pieces sprinkled around my home and I am all set to go!

Q: **How can I reinvent my space and fall in love with my home again?**

A: By changing out your accent pieces, of course! We all get in a funk sometimes and feel like we need to replace things in every room in our home. It's normal to feel that way. But can you imagine if the answer to sprucing up a room was to change everything out? No need to go that far! Simply think about switching two or three things in your room. Start with:

1. pillows
2. a throw blanket
3. a vase filled with new fresh or faux florals

And voila! You now have a room that feels completely revamped and fresh! You can, of course, take it a few steps further, but I wanted to share with you how it can be done minimally.

Looking for an easy way to redecorate for the season? **Change your color palette** to one that reflects the season like this plum and gray; it's perfect for fall!

THE BASEMENT

A basement is a basement . . . until you furnish it to look like it's not. I love my basement today but that was not always the case. This area was painted with a dark color and had carpet everywhere. It felt dingy and absolutely not welcoming. It was a wasted space that we never used because no one wanted to spend time down there. I decided to take action and make this floor an extension of the rest of my home, but I wanted it to be a fun hangout space for all of us to enjoy. Adults and kids alike!

Since the whole space is an open area, I chose to go with a consistent color palette that you see throughout the room: pastel hues of pink and blue. Fun yet very relaxing. I painted my walls a soft tone with a warm base: Perfect Greige at 50 percent by Sherwin Williams. Then I tore out the carpeting and had vinyl flooring that looks and feels like real wood installed. The color is perfect to brighten up this room, and the vinyl allows me to be completely and utterly worry free!

Q: How do I decorate around leather furniture?

A: A lot of homeowners opt for leather sofas and chairs. Leather is more durable and easier to clean than fabric, especially with kids or pets in the mix. So, I understand why you would want to pick leather over fabric. I also understand that you may feel lost when it comes to decorating around leather furniture.

Leather is pretty versatile with many colors. In order to tone down leather's masculine feel, I like to add pillows with metallic threads, beading, or velvet, which glams things up and softens the look while adding texture.

If you need added seating, bring in an armchair that's not leather. I am here to tell you that it's absolutely okay to mix leather with other fabrics like velvet or linen. Liven things up with patterns, warm things up with faux fur, and you will end up with an elegantly designed space for you and your family to enjoy!

Now that the main parts of the makeover were taken care of, I had to furnish. I divided the TV area and made it into a hangout spot for everyone. A sectional paired with a tufted ottoman were the perfect pieces for this space. We spend evenings down here playing board games or watching movies. To add storage, I placed a credenza under the TV for toys and knickknacks.

A few benches, armchairs, and wall art and I was done! We now have a cozy and fun space that has become everyone's favorite place to hang out.

To finish off my basement look, I added two gorgeous chandeliers for the touch of glam that I love so much.

I also styled a beautiful white wash cabinet against an empty wall and layered the space with a mirror and pretty decor.

With my kids getting older and their friends coming over constantly, I wanted to give them a space they could call their own. (And to keep them away from my main floor, but let's not share that with them . . .) On this side of the basement, I made a fun hangout spot for the kids with faux-fur beanbags, tufted ottomans, and a candy station for them to enjoy. But I have to share: Most adults who see this floor gravitate toward the beanbags first!

4

DINING AREAS

DINING AREAS

Dining room or kitchen nook? Or both? What's the difference? Good question!

A nook is a dining area that is connected to or part of your kitchen. It's typically used for daily meals but is also a great place for kids' arts and crafts, homework, or a place for you to catch up on your work. It's a very high-traffic area because of the constant use.

A formal dining room usually does not get as much use as a kitchen nook. It's normally used for more formal entertaining, when you pull out all your gorgeous dinnerware and host family and friends for the holidays or other special occasions.

If your home has one dining area and you have the space, invest in a rectangular table or oval table that extends for added seating when you're entertaining. If you do not have the space for that, try to go with a round table to avoid making your space feel cramped. FUN FACT: Did you know that a round table usually fits the largest number of diners in the smallest amount of space?

Built-in banquettes can be pricey, but they're another great space-saving solution. They'll maximize seating and can be designed with extra storage areas along the bottom.

SMALL SPACES

When considering dining furniture for your kitchen, think durability. In a small, busy area, glass can prove to be hazardous. I'm a huge fan of distressed wood for a kitchen nook table. The more scratches and dings, the more character you'll be adding. There are so many beautiful wood dining tables out there in a variety of different colors, shapes, and sizes. Shop around and see what catches your eye.

HIGHLIGHTS

Strategize based on how you'll be using your dining area.

Pick your table based on regular usage and room size.

Even a small corner can be turned into an elegant,
functional dining area.

REMEMBER

While some homes offer both a formal dining room and a dining
nook, others may have just one dining area for both everyday use and
entertaining. Either way, you can make these dining areas work for you and
your lifestyle. It's just a matter of being strategic about it.

CHECKLIST FOR DINING AREA SUCCESS

O Your dining table should fit your daily needs (as well as room size)

O Mix-and-match seating adds a fun twist; see the next page for options

O Lighting is key and should provide a range of options for every
   mood or time of day

O Rely on fresh or faux floral arrangements to add pops of color or
   to change things up

Opposite: A petite bistro table is a chic solution to small-space
dining areas.

Choosing your seating is fun because you can mix and match! Think side chairs and armchairs; chairs and a bench; armchairs and two benches . . . see? There are many ways to approach this! You can probably guess what I'll also recommend: Investing in seating that comes with durable or stain-resistant fabric. Especially if your seating is a light color—you want to be able to easily wipe down any spills without having a mini heart attack every time you have a meal. One thing I like to do for added protection is to ask my kids to place kitchen towels on their seats. Especially with younger kids, I've found this to be a great and quick way to protect dining chairs.

RUGS

Rug or no rug? This is totally a matter of preference. Personally, I love a rug. It warms up a space but also offers warmth under your feet when you're sitting at the table. Invest in a rug with a pattern if you're worried about staining. It hides any stains better once spot-cleaned. Keep a cordless vacuum accessible for quick and easy crumb cleanups between meals. But if you feel like a rug will be too much work and upkeep under your dining set, then skip the rug. You can't go wrong either way.

Q: How do I know what size area rug to place under my dining room set?

A: Interestingly enough, I've been asked this question so many times, and believe me, I get it. It's like a domino effect where one question leads to the next, and the next thing you know, you feel like crawling under your bedsheets and forgetting about the whole thing altogether. Second-guessing yourself is counterproductive, so try to avoid overthinking things. No matter the size of the area under your dining set, choose a rug size that will keep your table and chairs fully on the rug. A rectangular table that seats six should fit over an 8' x 10' area rug. A 5' x 7' rug is great for smaller, square dining tables that seat four. Go with a five-foot round area rug for smaller kitchen nook areas. When in doubt, reach for a measuring tape. I always have one within easy reach in my home. It makes decisions about certain things a lot easier—which means fewer returns! (Who am I fooling? I'm terrible at returns.)

If you have a large dining room, go big and bold with an extravagant chandelier.

LIGHTING

Lighting is a great way to add a touch of glamour and take your room to the next level. Choose a shape that complements your table for visual consistency. For example, hang a round fixture above a round table, and choose an oval or linear fixture to hang above longer and rectangular tables. Over the years I've heard this: "Round fixtures go with round tables, and linear fixtures go with rectangular tables." But, my friends, rules are meant to be broken! I've used a round lighting fixture in my dining room and love how it offsets the rectangular shape of the table. This speaks to the idea of "thinking outside the box." Remember to consider the size of your space. Scale is very important. If you have a large dining room, go big and bold with an extravagant chandelier. If your space is not that big, smaller fixtures will achieve a similar effect without taking up too much space and overwhelming your room. Most of the lighting in my home is from Lamps Plus. And that's the 101 on lighting in dining rooms.

Opposite: A bench is a great way to mix and match your seating and allows for up to eight adults to comfortably fit around the table. Looks good and serves a purpose.

And now for the finishing touches! In a kitchenette, you'll want to avoid overdoing it with decor because you'll want your table surface to remain accessible for your day to day. Think simple, like a flower arrangement, or a couple of hurricane candle holders on each side of the table!

Right: If you have space to add a credenza or cabinet, then consider yourself lucky! It's a great way to store your essentials and maybe even your children's arts and crafts! Style a mirror or wall art above your furniture piece. Add a few accent decor pieces on the credenza top and you'll have a kitchenette that looks nice and fits your lifestyle. And it makes a statement for you to enjoy every day! Visual appeal for yourself is always key. But if you have limited space, a console table styled with a piece of art is a great way to fill up an empty wall without taking up too much room.

DINING ROOM

In your dining room, functionality is not a top priority, unless you tend to entertain constantly. In here, you can get away with a glass-top table or even an all-mirror table. Just be sure to opt for a table that fits comfortably in the room, meaning you'll still have enough space to move chairs and walk around with ease.

Dining chairs with fabric protection are important for this room, too, but if you don't entertain too much and mainly adults get to eat in here, you can get away with no fabric protection.

Don't think twice about a rug in the dining room . . . it's a must! It will anchor the room and add a statement as well as texture and color.

Q: **How do you make a simple statement in a dining room?**

A: If you're looking to make a statement through your decor in a simple yet eye-catching way, think of floral arrangements for your centerpiece.

Flower arrangements are my go-tos for easy, natural, and arresting touches. I've never met anyone who didn't enjoy a few dramatic blossom branches styled in a vase, a collection of spring tulips, or even some faux greenery! The possibilities are endless here.

In my dining room, I love going all-out with my centerpiece. Because we almost never use the room, it's a centerpiece that stays put for long periods of time, so it's okay if it takes up most of my dining table. I can easily remove it when I need to set my table for a dinner party!

This is also a great place to have fun with wall decor! Art, mirrors . . . yes! Go for it and take this room to the next level! If you have a tight dining room, think of an oversized (or even leaning, maybe?) mirror on your wall or above your buffet or credenza to give the illusion of a bigger space.

SETTING A TABLE

Entertaining is exciting! With our busy day-to-day lives, it's nice to enjoy family and friends around a dining table filled with laughter, fun conversations, and love. It truly is all about the company, but why not elevate the experience for your guests with a beautiful tablescape for everyone to enjoy? Taking time to set my table with layers of dinnerware and silverware brings me back to my childhood, seeing my mom put so much thought into making sure her guests felt loved and appreciated through her special touches around the dining room.

You know all that beautiful dinnerware you've been saving? A special occasion is the time to whip them out, my friends. Think about the layering process . . .

❶ You could start off with a place mat and layer it with a charger (or service) plate.

❷ Add your dinner plate.

❸ Think about what you will be serving. Salad and soup or soup or salad? That is how you will decide if you will need a salad plate and soup bowl, or either/or.

❹ Your silverware comes next. The knife goes on the right, with the blade facing the plate. Place a soup and dessert spoon (if needed) to its right. The forks go to the left of the plate, arranged from smallest to largest.

❺ Wineglass or beverage glass goes on the top right.

Now that we have the base done, the fun begins! Through your centerpiece and napkins, you can add color and texture, and pretty much take the whole look to the next level.

1. Decide on a color palette. Then style the napkins and napkin rings over the dinnerware.

2. Take it one step further and add place cards to let your guests know where their seats are.

3. Finish off the look by adding a few candles or floral arrangements for a festive look to set the mood for the evening.

4. Often we can't fit all the food on the table, so think about buffet style. Set your food on the credenza in your dining room if you have one, or bring in a folding table and cover it with pretty linen before placing your food on the table for your guests.

5
KITCHENS

KITCHENS

Before you embark on a kitchen remodel, prepare yourself for what's ahead. Have you ever heard the saying, "If your marriage survives a kitchen remodel, then you know you're solid?" (Wait . . . is that a saying or did I make it up? Can't remember . . . but either way, it's true!) It's only one room, but it's the room that provides the essentials for your daily survival. So remember: When there are no functional appliances and you have construction workers walking in and out of your home, day in and day out, disrupting the basic routine that normally keeps your home and family going, this will cause tension and stress. (By the way, you may want to save a kitchen remodel for the summer, when you can survive using an outdoor grill, or be prepared to enjoy takeout for a while.) It will all be worth it when your beautiful brand-new kitchen is done! Also, look on the bright side, no cooking for a month or two . . . where do I sign up?

With kitchen trends and technology constantly evolving, it's no wonder most homeowners feel confused when it comes to designing a new kitchen. We want all the beautiful details plus the gadgets that will make life in the kitchen more efficient. Unlike a family room or bedroom, a kitchen remodel means whatever you choose for that room is a long-term commitment. Tile and counter choices are not easy to change out once installed. Cabinets can't be easily repainted or replaced if you decide you don't like the color. So it's important to take your time and think this through.

First, take a moment and sit down with a notepad and a pen. If your home includes a significant other and kids, make it a fun evening! Go around the table and have each person share what they would love to have in the kitchen. Okay, okay, I know the kids may come up with some crazy ideas but what's the harm in making them feel

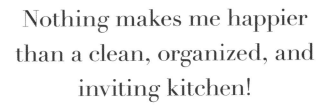

Nothing makes me happier than a clean, organized, and inviting kitchen!

heard and included in the process? You can always say, "Sorry, honey, the contractor said it would be impossible to add a bouncy house in here, so we'll have to pass. Good idea, though!" See? Easy! Always blame it on the contractor. On a serious note, making a list of what's important for your lifestyle will keep you focused on the overall goal and help narrow down what you do and do not need for your project.

A few years ago, I completely remodeled my kitchen. I like to cook and entertain, and our kitchen is often the place where people end up hanging out, especially my family. So, in addition to new, quality appliances, I wanted the kitchen to look organized, clutter-free, and inviting. Since I have an open-floor plan, it was important to me that our kitchen eating area flowed from our kitchen to our family room.

Are you going to keep the layout of your current kitchen or are you reconfiguring things for a better flow? Once you've figured this out with the help of your contractor, it's time for next steps.

Here is the order in which I tackled my kitchen renovation:

1. Cabinetry and hardware
2. Counters and backsplash
3. Flooring
4. Wall paint color
5. Appliances
6. Decor and accents

FINDING THE RIGHT CONTRACTOR

If you're embarking on a full kitchen or home renovation, you'll need a good contractor. And by "good" I mean someone who will listen to your ideas, be honest with you about how feasible they are (and how much they will cost), and be able to make recommendations or adjustments along the way. Interview several contractors before you decide, and ask for references. Here are some questions that you can ask former clients:

1. Did the contractor come in on time and on budget?
2. Were they courteous to you and your neighbors?
3. Did they facilitate getting the right permits, etc.?
4. Were they neat and careful throughout the entire process?
5. Do you have any regrets?

STEP #1:

Cabinetry and Hardware

Your cabinets are the first step toward achieving your dream kitchen. There are two ways to go about this.

1. You can sand down your existing cabinets and repaint them, which allows for a budget-friendly update. (I highly recommend you hire a professional or company that specializes in upgrading cabinets. It's worth the investment.)

2. Or, you can tear out your existing cabinets and purchase new ones. Visiting a local showroom can be very helpful if you choose to go this route. Take it a bit further and ask for samples to bring home, which is essential in helping you visualize what the cabinets will look like. The next step would be to get a drawing of the layout with the new cabinets to see how it will all come together. Most kitchen showrooms offer virtual imaging so you can see what your kitchen will look like. If you're working with an architect, they can do this too.

Picking the color of your cabinets can be easier said than done. I was looking for white cabinets and found out that saying "white cabinets" doesn't cut it. This was an aha moment when I realized there are waaaayy too many shades of white out there. Remember, it's all about the overall look you're hoping to achieve. Do you like dark and moody? Go with dark colors. Do you like light and airy? Go with light colors. Do you like a two-toned look? Then incorporate two-colored cabinets in your kitchen! Play around with samples and see what catches your eye. Don't forget to take samples home and lay them out to see how the colors work in your kitchen's natural lighting. Give it at least twenty-four hours before deciding. See how the colors look in the morning, midday, and evening light.

Since I live in Michigan, where winters can be long and gloomy, I knew I wanted to make my kitchen cozy and bright. These are all factors to keep in mind as you make your decision and finalize cabinets.

Remember when I said that details make a room? In a kitchen, your hardware is part of the details. Knobs and handles. Be very picky and take your time when choosing your hardware. They can definitely elevate your cabinetry. Have fun! Think of them as the jewelry in your kitchen.

STEP #2:

Countertops and Backsplashes

As beautiful as some kitchen counters are, try to focus on durability and daily upkeep. There are so many beautiful options out there (who doesn't love marble counters in the kitchen?), but they may not be practical when it comes to everyday cooking and cleaning. So do your research to figure out the best option for your lifestyle and budget. In our old kitchen, we had Corian countertops. We decided to change them out to granite, which is a sustainable, natural stone that comes in many different colors.

You can't go wrong using white subway tile as your backsplash. I see this look everywhere—because it's classic and complements any kitchen style, from farmhouse to modern.

When it comes to kitchens, remember to **focus on what you want and what makes you happy.**

STEP #3:

Flooring

When I was remodeling my kitchen, something I struggled with was what type of flooring to put in. Before the renovation, we had wood floors. I love the look of wood floors in any room, but in this high-traffic area, they were getting damaged with dents, scratches, and water damage from spills. (Engineered wood floors were not an option at the time.) After a lot of back-and-forth, we decided to go with tile. This is where I'll admit that even designers make mistakes! I now believe putting tile in my kitchen was the wrong decision. I learned—the costly way—that tile can crack. Also, the grout gets dark and looks dirty, no matter how many times we clean and seal it. The lesson to take away from this? There are always pros and cons with everything you put in your home. Focus on what you want and what makes you happy and fits your lifestyle.

Q: **Would you rather invest in flooring or countertops in a kitchen?**

A: That's a good question! I'd say countertops. They are more visible and can do more to elevate a kitchen's design. (They will also increase your home's resale value.)

There are many types of treated wood floors that look great and are easy to clean and maintain. There is no doubt that wood floors are warm and add so much texture to a room. If you're worried about damaging your wood floors in a high-traffic area like a kitchen, consider vinyl wood flooring, which looks exactly like wood but is durable, waterproof, and budget-friendly.

STEP #4:

Applicances

AHHH, the appliances. There was a time when appliances didn't matter much to me. Then I became a wife and a mom and realized my family needed food to survive—that's when appliances became an essential part of our kitchen. If you're anything like my husband, then you'll enjoy checking out reviews, price comparisons, and frustrating your significant other before committing to any appliance you need for your kitchen. When we were looking into appliances, my head was spinning from all the new technology out there. I just wanted a fridge that could keep my food cold and wouldn't break three years from now. Who can guarantee this? The answer? No one! So please make sure you invest in an extended warranty, my friends. Yours truly learned the hard way. I personally do not like to suggest appliance brands because there is no guarantee that your experience will be the same as mine (also learned that the hard way). So remember: Look for appliances that have the features you need, that are within your budget, and fit in your current kitchen. And get a warranty. Did I say that already?

STEP #5:

Decor and Accents

And so the fun begins! Remember, it's all in the details. Styling a kitchen with decor and accents is the finishing touch you'll need before you can do a happy dance! Remember not to overdo it, though, because you'll need the counter space for cooking. A few decanters, a decorative cake stand, and maybe even a coffee/tea station for you to call your own, and done. Have fun with it! I love styling a kitchen island with faux floral branches or fresh flowers. Add a candle and a tray and you now have a pleasing vignette.

Your kitchen should look good, but it also has to function for your everyday life. I'm a huge coffee drinker, so I decided to have fun with some counter space and use it as a coffee bar.

STYLING YOUR KITCHEN ISLAND & COUNTERS

You probably won't hear me say this phrase much: "Don't overdo it!" As much as I love styling my home, when it comes to kitchen counters, I try to keep my decor minimal so that I still have counter space to work on. In here, styling with kitchen items that you use every day could help maximize your decor. For example, use canisters to hold your wooden spoons and mugs for a fun design statement that still makes it easy to reach your everyday essentials. There are so many beautiful canisters out there. Choose a set that will complement the rest of your kitchen but will also help you organize and store everyday ingredients like flour, salt, and sugar. Layer cutting boards against your backsplash, and style a paper towel holder or even a faux greenery arrangement in front of it.

On my island there are four essentials I always have to add to my vignettes:

1. Vase with fresh or faux florals
2. Candle
3. Snacks my family and I love to enjoy on the days we're gathered in the kitchen
4. And, of course, a tray!

Don't forget your sink! Remember that excruciating chore called washing the dishes? Well, to make that chore a little more bearable, I styled a cute arrangement that includes a pedestal topped with a small floral arrangement, soap in a cute dispenser, and a candle. It makes doing the dishes so much more enjoyable!

BEFORE

AFTER

Here is a Before picture of a kitchen that needed a bit of sprucing up. The goal was to make the space feel updated by using decorative accents and replacing the counter stools. Easy and budget-friendly!

FAQ

Q: How can I spruce up my kitchen without having to go through a complete remodel?

A: I'm happy to report that not every kitchen needs to be gutted to get a refresh. Sometimes small changes can make a big impact, as you can see in these Before and After photos. Changing out your counter stools, installing a pretty vignette on your island, and adding a few decorative accents on your counter get you good to go!

6

BEDROOMS

BEDROOMS

AAHHHH, the bedroom! (Well, when you walk into your bedroom, it should make you say just that: Aaaahhhh!) I think it's crazy that this is usually the last room one tackles when designing a home. It's almost like it's the underdog of the house. But let's think about this for a second. Where do you start your day each morning? Where do you end up every night? And where do you generally spend the most hours? The answer to all these questions is the bedroom! Now, I have mentioned throughout this book that your home should be your oasis: It should spark that inner peace we all look for. Well, in this oasis your bedroom should be your primary sanctuary.

I believe having a well-designed bedroom can truly impact how you feel each morning, and it can set the tone for the rest of the day. Imagine waking up and one of the first things you do is make up a beautiful bed. Now you're feeling productive and ready to tackle your day. You get dressed and walk out the door. All throughout the day, no matter what you're doing, no matter how stressful your day becomes, what's the one thing you can look forward to? Curling up in bed under some cozy blankets, maybe with tea in hand and a book to read? Imagine walking into a beautifully furnished and decorated room, a neatly made bed waiting for you: AAAHHHH, heaven! Now do you understand why I think it's important to focus on your bedroom?

By the way, kids' bedrooms are no different. Every kid likes to retreat to their bedroom, whether it's to play, read, sulk, or enjoy a moment of privacy. As my children have gotten older, I've asked them to participate in styling their rooms. When my daughter wanted to transition her bedroom from a little girl's room to a big girl's bedroom, for example, she chose to add her (current) favorite color, turquoise, through accents and special decorative items. The result was a room she loves and feels reflects her personality. See more on kids' bedrooms on page 184.

HIGHLIGHTS

Keep to cozy, warm, neutral colors. Color accents can come in with pillows and other accessories.

It's perfectly okay to mix and match side tables.

Try to make your bed each morning! It will help get your day off to a good start, and it will be waiting for you in the evening.

REMEMBER

Don't make your bedroom an afterthought. You'll be spending a LOT of time in it, mostly trying to relax. So, make sure it's relaxing for you!

CHECKLIST FOR BEDROOM SUCCESS

○ Wall color
○ Bed and headboard
○ Dressers and nightstands
○ Additional seating
○ Pillows, blankets, accent decor

Your home should be your oasis, and *your bedroom should be your primary sanctuary!*

Here are my six steps to simplify the process and inspire your bedroom design. I'll also show you different ways you can display pillows on your bed, set up your bedding, and more.

STEP #1:

Paint

Paint is very important in the bedroom. My personal preference is sticking to lighter shades, which I think creates a relaxed feel in a room. If you prefer a darker color, that's also fine. Either go with one accent wall in a darker shade (usually the wall behind your bed), or, if you'd like to use a dark color throughout your room, go with lighter furniture and accents to balance out your color palette. The bedroom is also a great place to add wallpaper on a focal wall behind your bed.

Because kids tend to change their minds about favorite colors what seems like every other hour, I suggest painting their walls a neutral color. This way you can easily change things up through their bedding and accents as needed. I infuse their color palettes through their bedding, wall art, and other accent furniture pieces.

Q: **How can I refresh my bedroom for the seasons?**

A: Here are the top three items you can change out for a quick refresh:

1. bedding
2. decorative pillows
3. throw blanket

STEP #2:

Choose Your Bed

Do you want a fabric headboard? Maybe you're more interested in a frame? Plywood? Wood and fabric? There are so many options! Once you've decided which direction you'd like to go, order the bed and move on to the next step.

STEP #3:

Dressers and Nightstands

If you have room in your bedroom for dressers, then you're in luck. They're great for added storage. Add a mirror over your dresser (seriously, who doesn't like a mirror in their bedroom?) or artwork to complete the look!

Nightstands are an essential part of any bedroom. They're great for storage, and a perfect surface for table lamps and your other bedtime essentials. Here's an opportunity to get creative: Your nightstands do not need to match your bed or dressers. You can mix and match your furniture pieces to make a statement.

If you're tight on space and looking for ways to make your room feel bigger, place mirrors over your nightstands and dresser and behind your table lamp. Why? When you turn on your lamps in the evening, the mirror will reflect the light and make your space feel bigger and brighter.

STEP #4:

Bedding

I can't say this enough: Your furniture may be amazing, but if your bedding looks sloppy, it will detract from the whole look of your design. Think about what makes you want to jump in your bed and stay there forever. Is it a layered look? Maybe lots of pillows? Does a throw blanket on your bed make it look cozy? HAVE FUN! If you have a partner, now is the time to think about everyone's needs. For instance, my husband is a cold sleeper, which means he needs three blankets and a sweater every night to feel comfortable enough to sleep. Naturally, I am a hot sleeper and only need a light blanket. With that in mind, I go with a layered look in our bedroom (see how I make my bed on the next page). This way my husband has all the warmth he needs, and I have the look I love. Win win! (Well, if he could persuade me to style fewer throw pillows on the bed then that would be a win for him, but since we all know that's not going to happen, I still consider this a winning solution.)

HERE'S HOW I LIKE TO MAKE MY BED

Sheets, light quilt, comforter. Top with pillows you sleep on, shams, and, to finish it all off, decorative pillows and a throw!

There is nothing like layering a comforter at the foot of your bed to give a plush look that will make you want to jump back in! Fold it and place it horizontally at the foot of your bed. At the head, place the pillows you sleep on. Then place shams in front of your pillows. Then add in decorative pillows. This is where you can have some fun! There are so many ways to style the pillows on your bed. Mix in texture and different sizes! Sizes to think about: 24", 20", and 18" pillows. Lumbar pillows are also great to add to the mix. Did I mention that I consider myself a pillow queen? Just ask my husband!

Here is another way to
arrange decorative pillows.

STEP #5:

Seating

If you have space for extra seating, add a love seat at the foot of your bed, along with a side table or coffee table for a reading nook where you can drink coffee in the morning or watch TV. If you do not have enough room, you can still add a bench or ottomans at the foot of your bed for added seating.

TO TV OR NOT TO TV?

I know having a TV in the bedroom is an ongoing debate and I understand the reasoning on both sides. Personally, I did not want a TV in our bedroom, but my husband did. (It didn't help that we had this discussion a day after I gave birth to our daughter and I was still drowsy and out of it, but that's a story for another day.) I guess this is where we learned to compromise as a couple. I like our bedroom to be styled a certain way with accents like lots of pillows and glamorous touches, and he wants a TV. They say "pick your battles," so in the end we each got what we wanted. Don't tell him I told you, but I have to admit I now love having a TV in here. After a long day, it's nice to snuggle up and watch my favorite shows before bedtime.

STEP #6:

Decor Time

- **Lamps and ceiling lights** for added lighting and late-night reading.
- **Art or mirrors** over your nightstands to avoid having empty wall space.
- **A rug** that goes under your bed for added coziness, especially if you have wood or tile floors.
- **Window treatments** to warm up the room and block out the sunlight in the morning.
- **Candles and candleholders.**
- **Picture frames** with family photos.
- **Trays, bowls, vases, more pillows, and throw blankets.**

KIDS' BEDROOMS

As a child, I would sit in class and daydream about moving my furniture around in my bedroom. I would then doodle in my notebooks and draw what my ideal bedroom would look like. (Now that I think about it, my interest in home decor started at a young age!) Today, I truly enjoy furnishing and decorating kids' bedrooms. It's always so much fun, because my inner child comes out! Luckily for me, my kids love it as much as I do, and we've enjoyed decorating their rooms together. And when I say together, I really mean it: make sure to hear their ideas and opinions and make them feel involved.

Some of the questions I ask my kids are:

1. What colors would you like in your bedroom?
2. Is there a theme you would like to focus on?

If I'm shopping online or in a store, I narrow things down to two to three options for them to choose from, simply to make the process easier. Once we have everything we need, from furniture to decor, I make sure they're there helping me set up their rooms, and together we bring our vision to life. It's so heartwarming to see the excitement in their eyes. If you think your kids don't care about the the way their rooms look, this is where they'll prove you wrong. They really do care, and their happiness is proof of that.

Furniture that also serves as storage will help keep things organized and stowed away. My daughter Celine has a storage bench in her room that can be used as extra seating but is also a place to store throw blankets, books, and other knickknacks. My son, Adam, has storage ottomans that he also uses to fill up with all his toys.

Both my daughters are at an age when they need a vanity as well as a desk for homework. So I invested in office desks and hung mirrors over them. That allows for dual function: a desk for homework and a vanity for when they're getting ready to head out.

CELINE'S BEDROOM

When a child becomes a teenager, their tastes and preferences change dramatically. Suddenly, the word *cute* is not okay to use to describe them or anything in their lives. In the case of my young teen, we designed a space for her to enjoy that's transitional and feels a pinch less juvenile and more grown-up. Celine asked for a touch of pink in her bedroom and wanted lots of oversized flowers everywhere. She also wanted a hint of charcoal gray throughout.

Of course I like to make sure a child's bedroom is visually on point, but—just like a family room—storage and functionality are key.

Right: If you have a place for a dresser, that is great because kids need all the storage they can get in their smaller bedrooms. But if you do not, then invest in a nightstand that has drawers.

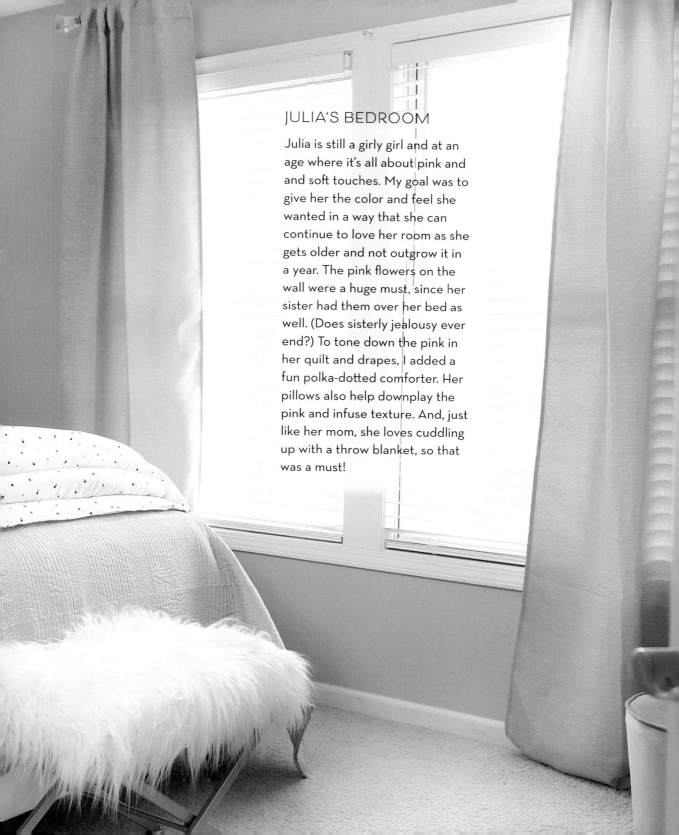

JULIA'S BEDROOM

Julia is still a girly girl and at an age where it's all about pink and and soft touches. My goal was to give her the color and feel she wanted in a way that she can continue to love her room as she gets older and not outgrow it in a year. The pink flowers on the wall were a huge must, since her sister had them over her bed as well. (Does sisterly jealousy ever end?) To tone down the pink in her quilt and drapes, I added a fun polka-dotted comforter. Her pillows also help downplay the pink and infuse texture. And, just like her mom, she loves cuddling up with a throw blanket, so that was a must!

Left: At the foot of her bed, a faux fur bench was a great way to give her a place to sit.

Right: Since we are limited with space in here, I got her a mirrored nightstand that also offers storage drawers.

ADAM'S BEDROOM

Oh, Adam. My son is all about Star Wars, just like his dad. Star Wars is very theme-y, but clearly even adults continue to enjoy it. So I wasn't too worried about him outgrowing his room anytime soon.

I don't think I've seen a kid as excited about a bedroom as he was when I revealed it to him a couple of years ago. Using the wall behind his bed as the focal point, I went with a fun hanging wall mural of hyperspace. His bedding definitely says Star Wars, so to tone things down, I added a plaid comforter to anchor it all. I knew I was going to be working with a lot of navy blue in here, so it was important for me to paint his walls light gray, which balanced out the dark tones.

With a four-year-old comes a lot of little toys! So storage here was very important. Adding storage ottomans made a huge difference and gave him a place to store away his toys when not playing. Also, my son LOVES reading! I knew I had to give him a bookshelf to organize his books. And the final fun touch? Well, a rocket ship tent, of course!

Q: How much should you let kids be involved in decorating their rooms?

A: I think it's very important to involve kids in the process of decorating their room (I'm talking ages five and up). Of course, you still have to take the lead, because, let's face it, kids will be kids, and their expectations can tend to be . . . ummm, unrealistic. But sitting them down and talking it through with them makes them feel 1) special and 2) that their opinion matters. This will help them love and appreciate their bedrooms—and maybe even encourage them to tidy them up from time to time!

Adam spends hours in his rocket ship tent reading. It's the perfect hideaway.

If you're going to go with a themed room, you might as well go all out, especially when it's for a younger child. It allows their imagination to run wild and gives them a fun and safe place to play in. It'll provide fun memories they will carry with them for years to come.

7

POWDER ROOM

POWDER ROOM

Is it weird to say designing a powder room gets me, um, excited? Well, it's true. A small bathroom is the one place where you can go absolutely crazy and get away with it. If you're eyeing a bold wallpaper but are afraid to commit to it in your main living space, use it in your powder room! If you're thinking of a dark or bright color palette but are hesitant or doubtful, go for it in the powder room! It's a small space that's tucked away, so use it to get that craziness out of your system! It's also the one room I think you should have fun with to let your guests see your funky side.

I actually designed my guest powder room two times before finally feeling like the project was complete. It was originally covered in forest-themed wallpaper by the builder. Can I say I just hated it? For lack of a better word, it was ugly. The first time around, I removed all the wallpaper myself (such a tedious process!), and painted metallic-gold and brown stripes around all the walls. The lesson I took away from that was to never again attempt to paint a bathroom alone. I repeat, I highly recommend hiring a professional for these types of tasks. As they say about painting, it's all about the prep work. Do not make my mistake and try to paint around a toilet seat and vanity . . . save yourselves, my friends.

Previous page: I wanted to do something I definitely couldn't in any other room and boy, did it pay off! This beautiful hand-painted wallpaper was exactly what I needed to bring my vision to life: texture filled with glitter and glam!

Opposite: My wood mirror matched the vanity. And then, for the grand finale: my crystal, over-the-top wall sconces!

Some of you may be thinking,
It's just a powder room. But I like
making my guests feel like
I've thought of everything for them.

The second time around, I added wallpaper I loved and switched out the vanity. But it was not making the impact I wanted it to. It looked good but was still missing something. So, I embarked on a mission to completely remodel the room again and promised myself this would be the last time.

I took a step back to really evaluate how I wanted to make the impact I was going for. Sometimes it's important to pause and try to understand all the ideas going through your head. Three important things to keep in mind when tackling this project:

1. Color palette
2. How to make a bold statement
3. Budget

I decided on black and brass (gold) as the color palette. I never in a million years thought I would use black textured wallpaper on all the walls in a room, but that ended up being my bold statement.

Next, I knew I had to find a vanity to not only fit in this tiny room but also to balance out the dark wallpaper. I searched high and low and couldn't find anything that would work. So custom was the way to go. I found a distressed hand-carved wood cabinet from a local store. After measuring, I had my handyman customize it by adding a marble counter, vessel sink (which sits on top of the countertop), and plumbing to create the vanity I envisioned.

I also wanted to add special touches for my guests. To achieve that, I styled hand towels on a tray for them to use. I purchased two matching soap dispensers and filled one with soap and one with lotion. I also included a perfume and cologne bottle on a tray and displayed extra toilet paper in case they ran out.

Some of you may be thinking, *It's just a powder room.* But I like making my guests feel like I've thought of everything for them. This is something my mom emphasized when I was growing up. She always made sure her guests felt welcome, loved, and appreciated, no matter who they were. It can feel strange being in a new environment when you walk into someone else's home. But knowing the host is going above and beyond always makes me relax and feel at ease. And it makes for a fun visit!

REMEMBER

A half-bath or small powder room is the perfect space to flip the script and design a unique, stand-alone space. Get playful with bright colors or patterned wallpaper, or go for darker tones like I did.

CHECKLIST FOR POWDER ROOM SUCCESS

○ Figure out what kind of impact you want in this room: bold and moody or soft and soothing?

○ Decide on a color palette

○ Start with paint or wallpaper

○ Vanity comes next; shop for a ready-to-go piece or go the custom route

○ Now think mirror

○ Light fixture

○ Hardware (toilet-paper holder, towel holder, etc.)

○ The final touches: wall art or decor, towels, soap dispensers, and anything else you need to add your special style!

My guests will easily find everything they need in the powder room. I like to offer hand towels, soap and cream, and perfume or cologne. Fresh flowers are always a nice touch and add a burst of color.

Right: Brass detailing through my handles, faucet, towel holder, toilet seat, and decor pops against the black textured walls!

In a powder room, you don't have to worry about displays with functionality to maximize your counter space like you would in your master bath. It's more about having fun and showcasing your creative side. Since you and your guests aren't using this room for daily routines like brushing teeth, applying makeup, doing hair, etc., you don't require a lot of gadgets and beauty products. You just need the essentials like soap and lotion.

With that said, it doesn't mean you can't display pretty vignettes to complement all that hard work you've done in this room!

* Brighten the small space with faux or fresh florals. It's visually appealing and a great way to add color.

* With all the options out there, choose dispensers and trays that tie back to your hardware and aesthetic.

* Layer trays with fun "bathroom themes." I like cotton balls or Q-tips in a jar!

* Who said soap had to be liquid only? I love finding fun-shaped soap bars and layering them on a pedestal (see opposite).

* And, of course, towels! Display your towels by rolling them and placing them on a tray, or layering them on the counter for an added special touch. Remember, practicality doesn't have to be the main focus here. Leave that for the master bathroom and kids' bathrooms!

GIRLS' BATHROOMS

Ah, teens and tweens. Girl teens and tweens, I might add! That wonderful age when they think they know it all, and routine mirror check-ins are a must. Does the hair look good? Did I apply enough lotion? Don't fight it, because it only gets worse as their daily routine needs grow, so accept it, my friends, and try to help them display their daily products in a more organized way. This will help keep their bathrooms tidy, help you keep your sanity, and avoid daily reminders to clean up. Oh, who am I kidding? But you get the picture.

I like to group the items they use on a daily basis on a pretty tray and keep it on their counter. It's there for them to use without having to look through their drawers. In the drawers and under-sink cabinets, I place everything else they need but not on a daily basis. I love using wicker baskets to keep their stuff organized. If I've learned anything, it's that the more you help them keep things tidy, the more you're helping yourself!

To finish off the look in this bathroom, I added a few fun pieces to reflect their personalities: a glitter art piece, cute butterfly towels, and feminine touches in their trays and dispensers. These are the ladies who love all the pretty things in their rooms, so I wanted to give them that in their shared bathroom, too.

she leaves a little
Sparkle
wherever she goes

she leaves a little

Sparkle

wherever she goes

Everyday products are usually organized on the bathroom counter. Non-everyday products I like to organize under the sink and in the vanity drawers. My go-to organizational tools are usually bins, baskets, and acrylic drawer organizers. They make it easy for my kids to find what they're looking for. They also help me help them stay organized.

BOYS' BATHROOMS

Adam is younger, and loves his Star Wars–themed bedroom. Since he has his own bathroom to enjoy, I painted and decorated this room to tie back to his bedroom color palette. Being so young, he doesn't have a lot of needs in here. Just the essentials for showering and brushing his teeth every day. So the organization is more for me than for him!

I went with a navy blue and gray color palette in here. I had the walls painted in navy blue and balanced them out with a gray-framed mirror and vanity.

I also added touches of blue and black through his shower curtain and Star Wars–themed wall decor.

I'm a big believer in baskets and bins to help organize my closets. They really help to reduce clutter, especially when it comes to keeping toiletries in one place.

ORGANIZATION

The linen closet . . . that closet that always finds a way to get messy and disorganized. Believe me, I know! I've had to deal with that craziness for years. I finally found a formula that works for me, and I hope you will find it helpful, too. I don't only organize towels and sheets in this closet, I also store away our everyday essentials so we always have extra at hand.

* To help keep my linen closet organized, I use baskets to keep things compartmentalized.
* Glass jars are also a great and stylish way to store smaller things if you have the room for them.
* I like to fold my sheets and towels and organize them by color.
* Use baskets to hold extra toilet paper.
* Linen closets are a great place to store your comforter and Euro shams when not in use.

8

WORK SPACES

WORK SPACES

Having a home office, whether it's a dedicated room or a corner carved out for a desk and chair, is essential for your daily life. It offers you a place you can work, catch up on email, pay bills, and keep life organized! My kids love to do their homework in my home office. They apparently feel all grown up in there. Never mind the fact that they have their own desks in their respective bedrooms. It's cute until they start forgetting their pencils on the office floor and I walk on a sharp pencil point and hurt myself. But again, that's a story for another day.

What are the essential furniture pieces for an office? A desk, an office chair, and shelves. Those are the major things you need to furnish an office room or space. With the way furniture design has evolved, office desks are looking more chic by the day. Think about it—when

Previous: My home office is set up so I can take meetings with clients or my kids.

Opposite: When it comes to kids, and if you have the room for it, dedicate a "kids' room" where homework and arts and crafts can take place! Not only will you help keep the slime and clay fun out of your main living space but your children will have their own room for storing away all their toys and arts and crafts. Think table and chairs rather than a desk. In this room, I've organized all their books, toys, coloring essentials, and more in a closet and dresser that I painted myself for them. This table serves as a place to do homework, work with their tutor, and do pretty much any fun activities their hearts desire.

you walk into an office, what's the first thing you notice? The desk! So take your time and pick the right piece that best reflects your taste.

Not all homes have dedicated studies or home offices. Here, strategy is important. Look around and figure out what wall or space you can dedicate to an office. You absolutely do not have to have a dedicated room for this. It can be in a living room, your family room, or even your kitchen area!

Next, move on to your office chair. Since I spend hours at my desk, a comfortable chair is important to me. I love a good wingback armchair for an office chair. But if you prefer a more traditional office chair, fear not! Office chairs have also evolved and now offer good-looking comfort.

With the amount of time you'll spend sitting at your desk, a rug can be a great addition to warm up the space visually and also physically warm your feet! And it's another way to make a personal design statement in your office.

HIGHLIGHTS

An office can be its own room or a desk tucked into a corner (see opposite).

REMEMBER

Organization is key to a successful working environment. This usually involves shelves and filing cabinets.

CHECKLIST FOR WORK SPACE SUCCESS

○ Bring in a desk and a chair. If you're styling against a wall, then think about artwork or a board to pin memos to hang on the wall above your desk.

○ Invest in a few organizational tools to keep all your paperwork and office essentials organized and looking good displayed on your desk.

○ Don't forget a pretty floral arrangement and a small table lamp for added lighting and cheerful styling!

No matter how you use your home office or how small your square footage, **your work space should work for you.**

An office needs a place to store . . . errr, style your books. If you have built-in shelves, then you're in luck!

If you don't, you can either invest in some shelves or even a credenza to help store your books and paperwork. Adding decor when styling your shelves is a great way to display your style and take your office from blah to fantabulous! Think fun bookends, decorative boxes, faux floral (for long-lasting styling), and picture frames to display precious family moments or awards and certificates.

In my book, you can never have too many light fixtures, even in a home office. It's the perfect statement piece and takes a room to the next level. It's also a great way to add a touch of glam.

If you have the space for them, add a couple of armchairs in front of your desk for those days when you have to carry on a meeting in this room. It's also a great place for your family members to hang out with you when you're working!

Don't forget wall art; it takes your walls from looking bare to adding that personal touch an office needs.

If you're working with little square footage, consider a two-in-one solution: a vanity that can also serve as a desk. Place a minimalist desk or side table against a wall in your room. Hang a mirror above, and finish it off with a chair. Now you have a desk that serves as both a work space and a vanity with a mirror.

9

OUTDOOR SPACES

OUTDOOR SPACES

Your front door is the first thing your guests see as they approach your home. We put so much time and effort into our indoor spaces, why not also include the front door and/or porch? As much as I would love to say what's on the inside matters more than what's on the outside, when it comes to home design, that's not necessarily the case. The front door should make a good first impression or impact in some way. I decided I wanted to offer my guests a welcoming hug before they even knocked on my door—and ever since, I have always taken the time to make sure I styled my front porch according to the season.

I'll share a secret with you, but let's keep it between us. One of my favorite things to do once spring hits is to take walks with my family around our neighborhood. Along the way, I love looking at how homeowners have styled their front doors or porch areas. When I see a beautiful front door, I immediately feel like the rest of the home must be showered with TLC, too. And I get so inspired by those who have taken the time to style this area; it makes me want to knock on their door and ask, "Can I please see what you've done with the rest of your home?" (So far I've managed to restrain myself.)

Previous page: My backyard has been transformed into an outdoor entertaining space. We love hanging out with family and friends out here. Memories we will always cherish!

Opposite: Outdoor lanterns are a great way to decorate and also infuse a warm and cozy evening glow. Set a couple of lanterns by your planters and you're one step further into styling this area!

I'm here to share that styling this outdoor entry to your home is as easy as 1-2-3. Given that it's a smaller space to work with, it's more about the styling and less about the furnishing. A few things can make a big impact.

Think:

1. Seasonal wreath/swag
2. Planters
3. Welcome mat

HIGHLIGHTS

You don't have to go overboard with your styling; a few pieces go a long way.

Planting seasonal greenery and flowers will take your front door from looking drab to fab!

REMEMBER

Your front door and porch are an extension of your home (and the first thing people see as they approach). These outdoor areas deserve as much care and attention as the inside!

CHECKLIST FOR OUTDOOR SPACE SUCCESS

◯ Paint your front door
◯ Choose tall planters for a dramatic effect
◯ Layer outdoor decor like lanterns, wooden signs, and fun orbs

APPLE ORCHARD
HOT CIDER
HARVEST FEAST
HAY RIDES
PUMPKIN
CORN

How can you make your guests feel welcome and loved at once, and how can you make this space scream "YOU"?

FRONT DOOR & PORCH

And voilà! You are now on your way to a fabulous-looking front door! However, I am someone who likes to glam it up, and you may have already said to yourself, *Hmmm . . . That can't be all there is to it, Farah!* Well, it can be if you just want an easy and effective spruce up, but no one ever said you can't take it one step further. Infuse your personality here and have fun! How can you evoke emotions? How can you make your guests feel welcome and loved at once, and how can you make this space scream "YOU"?

Maybe a couple of fun outdoor decorations to personalize this area can take your space from looking beautiful to looking fantabulously you! Look into some decorative accents to style in your planters for a personal touch. Maybe a few wood milk crates with seasonally appropriate decor would make for a great layering piece here. I am a huge sucker for those wood signs that say WELCOME and HOME. I also like string lights to make our front porch look festive.

If you have the space for it, add a couple of chairs or a bench on your porch for those days you and your family want to sit outside enjoying Mother Nature and seeing what's happening in the neighborhood. You don't need much more—maybe a small outdoor area rug, or a couple of fun accent pillows will do the trick. In the summer, I love drinking coffee on my front porch every morning. Quiet, peaceful, and serene.

Now you'll have the home people will ogle and appreciate as they pass by!

I have always loved offering my guests an experience when approaching my home. I style my front porch according to season.

Left: You don't have to go overboard with your styling. Pick out planters that complement the colors of your exterior.

Right: If you have a covered front porch, add outdoor pillows and a throw for those chilly nights when you want to cozy up outside! Lanterns make for warmer styling, as there's nothing like the glow of a candle.

OUTDOOR DINING

Oh, summer nights! Remember when backyards used to be endless visions of trees and grass? A few lawn chairs, maybe a bistro set, and call it a day. Boy, have we come a long way, ladies and gentlemen! Why? Because outdoor living has become an extension of indoor living. From outdoor kitchens with grills and sinks to fireplaces or firepits, our yards can be second kitchens or family spaces. Outdoor furniture is now made to replicate the comfort of indoor furniture.

If you live somewhere where it's hot all year, you're one of the lucky ones who gets to extend your living space outdoors all year long. If you're like me and live in an area where it's cold and dreary most of the year, outdoor living becomes a must in the summer. And we take full advantage of the warmer weather—nights filled with friends and family, dinners, barbecues, s'mores, and a drink or two.

Our backyard has truly become an extension of our indoors!

OUTDOOR LIVING SPACE

When we first moved to our home, I knew I wanted to tackle our backyard at some point. With all the other projects I had to focus on, this space was left at the bottom of my to-do list for years. When I finally got around to working on this project, I had so many ideas I wanted to incorporate in this makeover. We wanted a bigger space to hang out and entertain in. Once we had the space done and furnished, we were ready to rock 'n' roll! My husband, Will, was a bit hesitant at first. With our busy lives, he felt like we wouldn't spend that much time back here. Well, I'm happy to report that not only do we spend a lot of time out here, Will has said that he loves every aspect of the outdoor kitchen and seating area! Farah 1, Will 0.

One thing to keep in mind: just like our indoors, our outdoors also needs sprucing up. Pillows and accent decor can give it an updated look without having to spend too much money. Most stores stock fun outdoor pillows and accents months before summer comes around, which always works to our advantage! But, of course, think of recycling your old pieces here as well. A spruce-up doesn't have to mean fully changing everything out. Just a few key pieces will do the trick.

ADDITIONAL SEATING

As they say, the more the merrier! Outdoor seating options have come a long way, and I'm all for it! In addition to your traditional seating solutions, think of benches and swings. I love seeing my guests get excited about the outdoor swing under my deck—there is always an inner child in every one of us. Benches and love seats offer intimate seating but can look oh-so-cozy when you add a few pillows and a throw.

FLOWERS

You can't think of an outdoor entertainment space without lots of flowers and plants, right? Planters are an important factor to keep in mind when designing your ideal outdoor living space. I chose to go with floor planters as well as smaller planters to style on my coffee table and side tables.

Above: An outdoor fireplace was a must for us! My family and I love gathering around the fireplace during chilly evenings or days. Feeling the warmth as we laugh and bond is heavenly.

Opposite: S'mores, anyone? Adding a firepit back here was easy and quick! A run to Home Depot and we had everything we needed to build the firepit my kids always wanted. I finished off this area with rocking chairs and we were all set. I'm not sure why it took me so long to do this—happy kids, happy Mommy! May I add, happy tummy, mmmmm, more s'mores, please!

OUTDOOR GRILL

Trying to take full advantage of our outdoor space also meant equipping it with a sink and a mini fridge along with the grill. This outdoor kitchen allows us to thoroughly enjoy our outdoor space without having to keep running in and out of our home. We have everything we need right here—for the chef and for those enjoying the chef's work.

These easy vignettes are styled for a fun evening outside! I store everything away when it's time to go back in.

10
ROUTINES & RITUALS

ROUTINES & RITUALS

Routines are important for any household, not only to maintain your home but to help you enjoy it to the fullest. A messy home won't feel like a soothing refuge at the end of a long day. (Personally, a messy home makes me feel unproductive and anxious.) As important as it is to decorate and design your home, keeping it clean and organized will contribute to a sense of inner peace and outward calm. That's why cleaning routines are a part of my everyday life.

Q: How do I keep my home clean and spotless with kids?

A: There really is no secret. I have daily and weekly cleaning routines that I try to stick to. Of course there are days when I just want to crawl into bed and completely ignore the mess. Give yourself some slack and don't be hard on yourself.

Previous page: I try to tidy up my kitchen each evening before I go to bed.

Opposite: After I clean a room, I light a candle in it to congratulate myself on a job well done. It makes me want to stay in the room and enjoy it a while longer.

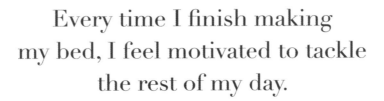

Every time I finish making my bed, I feel motivated to tackle the rest of my day.

HIGHLIGHTS

With the kitchen being such a high-traffic area, brighten the room with fresh flowers. Consider tall branches on your island for a dramatic look. Yes, please!

When I cook or clean, it's always fun having flowers and a lit candle to make these tasks a lot more enjoyable, and it puts a smile on my face as I go about my day in the kitchen.

REMEMBER

Establish a routine for easy cleanups and go for bigger projects when you get a chance. I like to tidy up throughout the day to avoid a complete pileup of work at the end of the day or the next morning.

CHECKLIST FOR ROUTINE SUCCESS

- ○ Make your bed in the morning
- ○ Organized closets and drawers make putting items away easier
- ○ If you can't tidy up before leaving the house in the morning, try to do it before going to bed
- ○ Reward yourself for your hard work

DAILY ROUTINE

Making my bed every morning

As rushed as I may be, I try to take a few minutes to make my bed each morning. This simple task gets my day started on the right foot. When I'm done, I feel motivated to tackle the rest of my day. No matter how stressful my day gets, I know I have a neat bed to look forward to collapsing in. Want to laugh at me? I cannot, for the life of me, get into a bed that's messy. You heard me. If for some reason I don't get a chance to make my bed in the morning, I will make it in the evening—even a few minutes before getting into it. It may sound crazy, but hear me out. I've found that getting into a bed that's messy and unmade at bedtime results in restless sleep. To me, it's definitely worth the few minutes to tuck in my sheets just so I can mess them up again.

Emptying the sink and tidying up the kitchen before going to sleep

Every evening before bedtime I make sure to load the dishwasher and tidy up. There's nothing like the feeling of going to sleep knowing I'll be waking up to a clean kitchen—especially an empty sink! Growing up, my mom used to say, "If you go to sleep and your home is messy, angels won't visit." She made sure her home was always in order before she went to sleep. This, ladies and gentlemen, is an example of how you become your mother's daughter. Let this be a lesson: Your kids do listen!

MAKING MY MORNING COFFEE

No fancy coffee machines here—just me and my handheld milk frother. I grew up watching my mom make her coffee this way and serving it to her guests. Now, as an adult, it has become an essential part of my morning routine.

① Warm up your choice of milk in a small pot.

② While the milk is warming up, add one heaping tablespoon of instant coffee of your choice in a mug.

③ Once the milk is warmed up (you'll know it's ready when it starts bubbling up on the sides), pour about a quarter cup in your mug.

④ With a handheld milk frother, mix the milk and coffee.

⑤ Gradually pour in a little bit more of the milk as you continue to mix with your frother.

⑥ Enjoy!

CLEANING ROUTINE

Let's face it, no matter how beautiful your home is, cleaning it is never fun. To make cleaning a bit less excruciating, I have a routine and a reward system in place that makes the whole process . . . dare I say it? Eeeenjoyable!

I hear this over and over: When it's time to clean, you feel stressed, you don't know where to start, and you give up before you begin. I hear you! Here's how I make the process less overwhelming: I take things one step at a time.

I tackle my cleaning one room at a time, one step at a time.

Try it; you'll thank me later! For example, I usually start in the family room. I start by fluffing up my pillows and properly styling them. Then I move on to styling my throw blankets. My coffee table is next. I wipe it down and put back my decor after dusting each piece. I go around and dust the rest of the decor in the room. I finish by vacuuming, and voilà! All done! (Well, almost.)

A few years ago, to keep myself motivated, I added a reward system to my routine. When I'm done cleaning a room, I light candles in that room and turn on my lamps. Seeing the room so clean and cozy motivates me to keep going. See more about this on page 276.

DID YOU KNOW?

I was surprised by the huge response I got after sharing my cleaning routine on Instagram. My followers said they felt motivated to clean while watching me do it—now it's become something we do together.

If you know anything about me by now, you know I love my coffee — and having a coffee station on my countertop is a luxury!

ORGANIZATION

Speaking of functional spaces, keep your drawers and pantries as organized as possible.

There's nothing like having everything clean, organized, and in its place. As my Instagram family knows, I clean my home on a regular basis, but I also believe in a deep spring clean each year. Spring cleaning can be tackled over one day or over a weekend, or maybe over the course of a few weekends.

My drawers are pretty well organized, mostly because I've learned to rely on containers. Look at my tea drawer, at right: Thanks to various organizers, I can easily see what types of teas I have and select one without having to root through boxes. I can also tell when I'm running low on a particular kind.

Every spring, I like to pull everything out of each drawer so I can wipe it down. I use hot water, mild dish soap, and a microfiber cloth. Once the drawers are clean, I bring in some fresh liners, cut them to size, and place them in the drawers. Then I put everything back, and I'm ready to go for another year.

MARRIAGE
is a relationship
in which one person
is always right and
the other is the
Husband
Behind every
GREAT
MAN
is a woman
rolling her eyes.

My pantry used to have metal wire shelving that I didn't love. It felt like I was always disorganized, and it didn't give me the space I needed. So I had the metal shelving removed and replaced it with wood shelves.

To thoroughly clean the pantry, I remove everything from the shelves and wipe them down with warm water and mild dishwashing soap. Then I vacuum and wipe down the floors with a swiffer, because, let's be honest, in pantries, the first thing you're going to have to deal with is accumulated crumbs and spices.

Getting organized is the part I love—removing everything from the shelves and taking stock. This is an opportunity to throw away all the expired items you didn't realize were expired, and to throw away things you no longer need, like those marshmallows you used to make hot cocoa in the winter.

Then you'll need to figure out what type of organizational tools you need. I got mine from a variety of stores, like Bed Bath & Beyond, Home Goods, Target, and the Container Store. Here are some of the things I find beneficial:

Glass canisters in different shapes and sizes. I store everything from flour, sugar, and other dry goods to crackers, pretzels, and other snacks and treats for my kids.

An expandable, tiered organizer, perfect for canned goods and spices, so you can see exactly what you have instead of losing track of whatever's in the back of the shelf.

A lazy Susan. I found a marble-topped one at Bed Bath & Beyond that's supposed to be for a dining table, but I thought it was perfect for my pantry. I put oils and vinegars on it.

Clear containers are amazing, and can be found anywhere. I store pastas and legumes in mine.

Baskets are another great storage solution, especially for garlic, onions, and potatoes.

If you use a lot of spices, consider buying matching jars. You can simply empty out your spices into the jars, label them, and place them on a tiered shelving unit so it acts as a spice rack in your pantry.

Before you start filling up all your containers, make sure you wash them. Once you've put everything into the baskets, canisters, jars, containers, or whatever organizational tools you've purchased, you can enjoy a pantry that will help you stay organized!

REWARD SYSTEM

I know it may sound a bit insane that we need to reward ourselves for doing what needs to be done, but I've always believed that you should do what you need to do to get yourself motivated. Now as much as I love a clean and tidy home, I find the process of cleaning it a bit tedious, and, like most, I often feel like crawling back into bed when my home is a huge mess. But looking forward to rewarding myself with something that makes me feel good inside, something that sparks happiness in me, makes the process more enjoyable. Because now I'm focusing on the end result. It helps me shift perspective. Instead of thinking *Oof! I need to clean*, I look at it as more of a treat for myself, because I truly enjoy the feeling I get once I'm done. For me, turning on lamps and lighting up a candle in each room is my reward. You can make your reward system whatever will motivate you! Some of my Instagram family have shared with me that their reward is a glass of wine when done, or a serving of their favorite treat.

STYLING FLOWERS

I am a HUGE sucker for floral arrangements. Ask my family—they'll definitely tell you I need to tone it down a bit. But what do they know? The moment a floral arrangement—faux or real—is added to a room, the space instantly feels more cheerful and vibrant. Flowers are a small addition with a big impact! So, no matter what my family may think about my floral arrangements, I maintain that I'm simply looking to add a cheerful touch wherever I can.

One of the questions I get repeatedly is, faux or real? Both, I say! I love and style either. Of course, there are pros and cons to consider here. For example, the faux florals that look and feel real can get pricey. On the other hand, it's a one-time payment and then you'll have them to style for as long as you wish. Real florals, of course, do not last very long. There are some tricks I'll share with you that can help with this, but at some point, fresh flowers will start losing their petals and wilt. However, since nothing compares to the look and smell of fresh flowers, I use them when I can, all year round.

Styling your own floral arrangements for your home is easy and fun. Therapeutic, even! For fresh flowers, I usually hit my local florist or buy them from my local supermarket. For faux floral stems, check out your local arts and crafts stores or even small decor boutiques.

To begin, you need the right vessel (or vase or bowl).

Q: **But really, faux or real?**

A: I say whatever your heart desires! There is no right or wrong here. It's a matter of preference. Personally, I like to mix it up. Sometimes you'll find me using faux floral stems, and other times I love taking the trip to my local floral shop and looking for fresh flowers to style in an arrangement. Faux florals have come a long way, and look and feel more and more like the real deal!

I love styling two vases of different heights filled with flowers, especially when it comes to tulips. The mix of all the bright colors and the high-and-low effect makes for a fun vignette!

STYLING FRESH FLOWERS

Add water to your vessel.

Trim your floral stems at an angle, and try to trim them between the nodes. Here's a trick I learned to make flowers last longer: Take a sharp knife and peel back the green part of the stem (on the bottom) to expose the inner white part. This is the part of the stem that absorbs water, so it helps to keep the flower fresh and alive for a longer period of time. Be sure to change the vase water every few days.

There are many other tips out there for keeping flowers fresh longer; most involve mixing sugar into your vase water. Here are a few:

1. Mix two tablespoons apple cider vinegar and two tablespoons sugar into the vase water

2. Mix in a little clear soda (like Sprite), or even a few drops of vodka along with sugar to keep bacteria from growing in the water

3. Throw a few pennies in your vase (also for bacterial prevention)

If your vessel is too wide, place tape on the top like this, which will help hold the stems in place. Then you won't need as many flowers to fill the vase.

Now have fun! Here are three ways I style fresh flowers.

STYLING FAUX FLORALS

Just like fresh flowers, faux florals also need the right vase or bowl. Are you looking for a full-flower look, or are you looking for the floral branch look? Here's a way you can style faux floral branches in a vase and a way to style faux flowers in a vase and bowl.

ACKNOWLEDGMENTS

It takes a village, they say, and boy are they right! I wouldn't be where I am today without, first and foremost, God and my ever-so-loving and supportive family. My parents, Jamal and Wafaa Baydoun; my husband, William Merhi; my kids, Celine, Julia, and Adam; my sweet sister, Faten; and my amazing brother, Mike. They have been a huge part of my life, shaping me into who I am today.

Along the way, I've been blessed to have the most amazing people support my dreams and help me achieve my goals. To Ahmad and Michelle Chebbani, you allowed me into your home and into your family when I first moved to the United States to attend college. You showed me that family has to help family, even those we've never met. I hope you know that welcoming me into your home as I started my new life here allowed me to spread my wings. Thank you!

To Fouad Baydoun, thank you for being like a brother to me.

To my agents: Brian Samuels, thank you for understanding me, for believing in me, and for making this a reality, and Erin Dippold, I love having you in my corner, helping me represent my brand.

Ted Larkins, you took a chance on me when you chose to sign me on as a client; thank you!

Thank you to Michele Winner, who believed in me at QVC: you helped make my dream of a home product line a reality.

To every vendor who took a chance on me and helped me with my product line, thank you! Adam from FHE, Chaya from TOV Furniture, Eric, Mina, and Steven from Nourison, and Julia and Jennifer from Tempaper.

To Simon & Schuster, Theresa, and Anja, and the whole Tiller team, I cannot even begin to tell you what this opportunity means to me. You listened to my vision for this book, you heard me, you understood me, and you helped this woman realize a lifelong dream. I will forever be grateful!

To my sisters-in-law, Sarah and Linda, thank you for being you.

And to every single friend and person who has been a part of my life and helped shape me into who I am today. There are so many, but you know who you are.

A special thank-you to Eastbrook Homes and Knoll Townhomes for allowing me into their beautiful builds for additional photography.

ABOUT THE AUTHOR

Farah Merhi is a designer, author, entrepreneur, social media influencer, and the founder and CEO of Inspire Me! Home Decor. It all started in 2012 as a creative outlet. Farah had a clear vision of what she wanted to do: inspire others and give them the tools they needed to make their houses into beautiful homes. She believes one's home should be a source of inner peace. She continues to inspire today with her beautiful home decor line and furniture collections. Farah launched an exclusive line that can be found only on QVC. She also has a home decor and furniture collection on Wayfair. Farah works hard to make decorating one's home simple, enjoyable, and affordable, whether through her book, her home collections, or her social media platforms. As an influencer in the home-decor space, Farah proudly works side by side as brand ambassador for successful and trusted brands. Being a wife and mother to three children, she knows that everyday life can be hectic; everyone deserves a personal sanctuary to walk into at the end of a long day.

ABOUT INSPIRE ME!
HOME DECOR

Inspire Me! Home Decor is a home-decor lifestyle brand that makes classic, elegant, and glamorous design accessible to homes around the world. Founded in 2012 by Farah Merhi, Inspire Me! began as an Instagram page and has since become the most-followed home-decor page on the platform, with over 5 million followers. Inspire Me! follows the curation and vision of its founder, embodying Farah's distinct style, passion for design, and connection to her audience. Inspire Me!'s digital platform is a go-to source for design enthusiasts ranging from housewives and self-proclaimed DIYers to designers and young professionals.